EDITH VELMANS

Edith's Book

VIKING

VIKING

Published by the Penguin Group
Penguin Books Ltd, 27 Wrights Lane, London w8 5tz, England
Penguin Putnam Inc., 375 Hudson Street, New York, New York 10014, USA
Penguin Books Australia Ltd, Ringwood, Victoria, Australia
Penguin Books Canada Ltd, 10 Alcorn Avenue, Toronto, Ontario, Canada m4v 3b2
Penguin Books (NZ) Ltd, Private Bag 102902, NSMC, Auckland, New Zealand

Penguin Books Ltd, Registered Offices: Harmondsworth, Middlesex, England

First published 1998
1 3 5 7 9 10 8 6 4 2

Set in 11/13¹/₂ pt Monotype Sabon
Typeset by Rowland Phototypesetting Ltd, Bury St Edmunds, Suffolk
Printed in Great Britain by Clays Ltd, St Ives plc

A CIP catalogue record for this book is available from the British Library

isbn 0-670-88161-9

For Anya, Jack, Nicky, Saskia and Luca

It's strange how much you can bear, if your doom is parcelled out to you in small doses. It's just like poison: if you start taking it very gradually, increasing the quantity drop by drop, then your body will eventually get used to it.

DAVID VAN HESSEN, MAY 1943

Contents

CONTENTS

Author's Note

When I came to live in the United States some twenty years ago, I was startled at the keen interest people seemed to take in what had happened to me in the Netherlands during the Second World War. My friends' curiosity about what to me had always seemed rather commonplace served to overcome my initial reluctance. I decided the best way to begin answering their questions and to tell my story was to translate my wartime diaries and letters.

The historian Dorothy Lipson and the writer Kati David, both dear friends, were the first to urge me to write down this story. It is a great regret to me that they are no longer here to see the fruition of their faith and encouragement.

Without the prodding, enthusiasm and professional expertise of my daughter Hester, I would never have been able to create order out of the chaos. Working together on this book was a wonderful experience for both of us. 'In editing your memoir,' she told me, 'I am learning to love and intimately appreciate the grandparents I never knew.'

For their help and friendship I also wish to thank Renata Laqueur, Wanda Fleck, Estelle Leontief, Marianne and Jon Swan, Karen Polak and, last but not least, for his wisdom and support, my husband of the past forty-nine years, Loet Velmans.

Edith Velmans

Prologue

It is July 1950. I am lying in a hospital bed in Amsterdam, my two babies in my arms. My doctor tells me the odds of having twins are just one in seventy-eight. He says this as if it's quite an achievement. An instant family! Sure, I think to myself. If I keep having two at a time, we can have the world repopulated in no time.

When I hear numbers like that I can't help thinking of the grimmer statistics. Of the 140,000 Jews in Holland before the war broke out ten years ago, fewer than 30,000 have survived – about one in five. Of the six of us in my family, two are left.

A few moments after the first baby was out and I was lying there exhausted, Dr Herzberger leaned over me and said hopefully, 'There's *at least* one more in there.'

After a long hard labour, I had no patience for the doctor's sense of humour. '*Ach laat maar zitten*,' I groaned. Which means: 'Oh just leave it in there, then.'

But it was no joke. Twenty minutes later another full-term, six-and-a-half-pound baby was born.

After Loet, the beaming father, had gone home for a few hours' sleep, Aunt Tine suddenly appeared at my bedside. She was the first to be allowed in – well before the visiting hour. She told the nurses she was the grandmother. She hugged me with tears in her eyes, and I was very moved.

Now it is the next day, and I am having a cosy chat with

the new mother in the bed across from mine. Her name is Miep Gies, and she is radiant. She is holding a baby boy – Paul. She tells me how she and her husband Jan had been longing for this moment. She is fifteen years older than me, and has been waiting a long time for a child. 'We got married, and then the war intervened – you know,' she says.

'I know,' I say, nodding.

The nurses walk into our room and start showing us how to put our babies to our breasts. I look round and ask the nurse, 'But what should *I* do?' The nurse says calmly, 'The same as everyone else!' 'Who, me? But, I mean . . . I've got *two*!' 'You've got two breasts, haven't you?' she says sensibly. 'Well then!'

Much to my astonishment, it works. I breast-feed my two babies, one at a time. When the other mothers have finished and can lie back and rest, I have to start all over again with the other twin. But we do it honestly, fairly, alternating breasts so that one will not have more than the other.

The days in the maternity ward fly by. Miep Gies and I compare and admire each other's babies, do stomach-tightening exercises together, giggle like schoolgirls behind the strict nurses' backs and exchange confidences. After being introduced to Aunt Tine and hearing me explain how exactly she is related to me (Tine zur Kleinsmiede is the woman who hid me from the Nazis during the war), my new friend Miep tells me that she, too, helped to hide a Jewish family, right here in Amsterdam. She stops and bites her lip, staring out of the window.

'What happened?' I ask softly. Not that I can't guess.

'They were betrayed in the end. 1944. We don't know by whom. Only Mr Frank came back from the camps. They had two daughters – Margot and Anne.' She dabs at her eyes.

I sigh. It's a familiar story. Everyone you meet has lost someone in the war.

Another day Miep sees me scribbling in the baby book I have enthusiastically begun for the twins.

'Oh, Anne was always writing too,' she says. 'You know, Mr Frank's daughter. She always said she wanted to be a writer when she grew up. She kept a diary. After the Nazis came for them, I took it and saved it for her. Now Mr Frank has had it published.'

'Really!' I say politely. 'I'd like to read it some day.'

I don't say this to Miep, but I don't think that very many people will be interested in reading this poor girl's diary. Lots of people must have kept diaries during the war – I know this because even I kept a diary. I have a suitcase full of journals dating from the war years. Anne Frank's story must be much sadder than mine, of course, because she died. Yet even she was just one of the thousands – no, millions of victims.

I sigh. In postwar Holland, nobody likes to talk much about the war any more. We who are left are too busy rebuilding our world to dwell on the past. We are just trying to get on with our lives as best we can.

Miep Gies's little boy Paul is constantly hungry. Miep has been having trouble breast-feeding, as her milk has not come in abundantly enough. I, on the other hand, am lactating like a leaky tap. Because I am spending twice as much time breast-feeding as the other new mothers, my glands are over-stimulated and produce so much milk that I have to stuff little glass receptacles into my bra to catch the overflow.

The nurses have come up with a most practical solution. When Miep's baby is crying because he is not satisfied, they collect my excess milk and give it to him in a bottle.

Miep is allowed to leave the hospital after ten days, while I, as the mother of twins, have to stay another week. Miep and I part as friends for life. Jan Gies, Miep's husband, returns every day to the hospital to collect my milk for his son. When

I am finally allowed to go home, we continue the routine for another two weeks. Finally little Paul's appetite levels off, and Jan's visits to our apartment, armed with his milk bottle, cease.

I don't get round to reading Anne Frank's diary until years later, when Anne has become a legend in the world.

There is another Miep in my life – Miep Fernandes, my best friend from school. It was to this Miep that I gave my diaries for safekeeping the day before I went into hiding. They were packed neatly into my little black patent leather suitcase. Actually, the suitcase wasn't really mine, it was Omi's. It used to contain the folded white lace-trimmed linens (chemise, robe, socks and bonnet) that my grandmother intended to be buried in. When the Germans invaded Holland and Father instructed each of us to pack up our most precious belongings in case we had to make a run for an air-raid shelter, Omi's suitcase was the only thing I could find that was just the right size. I appropriated the suitcase for my journals and dumped Omi's funeral clothes unceremoniously into a drawer.

After the war, Miep Fernandes returned the little black suitcase to me, with its precious contents intact: my diaries, with their cheerful striped and gingham covers. I have kept them all these years, through countless moves and life changes. My first diary is the most serious-looking of the lot, brown leather tooled with gold. This is what it says on the opening page:

19 September 1938
This book was given to me by my grandmother, Omi, when she came to live with us with all her trunks and boxes from Germany. So you could say this is a piece of my inheritance! I will use it as a scrapbook, so that later, when I am grown up and we are living in another era, I'll be able to recall

these 'modern times' in which we live now, and laugh about the funny and old-fashioned things we thought were the latest thing in 1938.

Sometimes I take out these early diaries and leaf through them. It gives me the kind of comfort a miser must feel when counting out his coins. I remember the urgent feeling I used to get sometimes to write things down, an urge I once tried to describe like this:

There are times when I'm so happy that I think I'm going to burst. I want to hold on to those moments – I want to catch, keep, and freeze them for ever. Like sun-rays in a little box that I can open when it's dark outside.

Here are my sun-rays, and my little box. How could I have foreseen that some day I would be needing them so much?

1

The Pear Tree

My grandmother, Mina Weil Wertheimer – Omi – came to live with us in 1938. She came from Sinsheim, a village near Heidelberg in Germany. Having lost one baby in childbirth and another to childhood illness, she had the misfortune of losing her husband – my grandfather, Gustav Adolf Weil – when her two surviving children were very young. The biggest tragedy of her life, however, was the death of Julius, her only son, who was drafted into the Kaiser's Imperial Army in 1914 at the start of the First World War. I remember the photograph on Omi's desk showing a handsome, proud Prussian officer with a thick moustache and wearing a spiked helmet. Next to the photograph was displayed a small iron cross, with '1914–1918' emblazoned in the centre. This was the *Ehren-kreuz* (Cross of Honour), awarded to all 'heroic mothers' who had sacrificed their sons for the *Vaterland*.

My mother, Adelheid Hilde, was the only child left, and Mina's only consolation: a dutiful and loving daughter. She had just graduated from school when the First World War broke out, and she spent the war nursing wounded soldiers returning from the front. It wasn't long before the end of the war that she fell in love with David van Hessen, a visiting Dutch businessman thirteen years her senior. In 1918, when Germany had been vanquished, Father brought Mother home to Amsterdam.

I have only vague memories of my grandmother's house in

Sinsheim. Behind the main house there was a separate building housing the laundry. This must have made quite an impression on me, because what I remember most vividly are the strong, red, bulging arms of the plump, motherly maid who boiled bedlinen in a large pan while scrubbing pillowcases and featherbed-covers on a metal washboard. 1 also remember the fragrant smell of apples lined up on slatted open shelving stacked high in the laundry attic. And I remember helping Omi pick redcurrants in the garden and then licking out the pan in which the jam had been made.

By 1938, the year my parents finally managed to persuade Omi to leave Sinsheim, she had been stripped of her German citizenship. She was Jewish; in other words, no longer acceptable. Her neighbours in Sinsheim avoided her, and even good friends regarded it as too risky to acknowledge her. Even so, she found it hard to tear herself away. My parents talked her into leaving her home by assuring her that nothing like this would ever happen in Holland.

Mother went to help Omi pack her belongings and 'sell' the parental home, although for all intents and purposes the house was confiscated. Someone had offered Omi a pittance for it, and Mother had been told it would be dangerous to refuse, or to haggle over the price. Mother reported that one or two 'Aryan' neighbours had sneaked in under cover of night to say goodbye. They told Omi they were sorry they couldn't visit her openly or even nod to her in the street. After all, fraternizing with Jews was now forbidden.

Omi was the first of a stream of refugees, many of them relatives on my mother's side, who found a warm welcome in our home, and often financial support as well, before going on to England, the United States or South America. Some of them even considered remaining in Holland. Naturally I thought this the best decision. Surely no other country in the world was a better place to live in than ours. After all, Father had told me that during the war of 1914–18 many refugees had found a safe haven right here in the Netherlands. When I was much younger, if I didn't finish the food on my plate, Mother would tell stories about the war years in Germany, when they had had little or nothing to eat. She was always talking about her 'entrance into Paradise' when she came to Holland as a bride and could suddenly get anything she wanted, even chocolate and oranges.

Well! That settled it, for me. It proved that our country was preferable to any other country on earth. Imagine living in a place where they didn't have any chocolate! Holland was a neutral country, that's why we had not participated in the Great War of 1914–18, even when some of the most deadly battles had been fought just across the border, in Flanders. If, as Father thought, Hitler tried to start something, we'd surely be safe here.

The German relatives caressed me, they pinched my cheeks and debated heatedly whom I resembled most. Their sentimentality was alien to me. In Father's family everyone was very sober, undemonstrative and down to earth. The van Hessens came from Groningen, in the north of Holland, where they had lived, first as cattle merchants, then as respected shopkeepers and businessmen, for generations. I felt slightly superior to these poor, deferential refugees who had lost everything and were facing an unknown future. I was secure in my happy, comfortable life in The Hague. I was proud to be a student at the Netherlands Lyceum, a prestigious private school.

Omi cried often, and I sensed that suffering meant a lot to her. Her departed ones were very much a presence in her life. She often stayed in bed with cold compresses on her head, for she had recurring headaches. I felt she used the headaches to manipulate my parents whenever she thought she was not getting enough attention. Mother spent a great deal of time tending to her; consequently, I grew resentful that I always had to share my mother with Omi. It also bothered me that since Omi's arrival, German was heard so often in our Dutch home. I hated that language, and like most people I knew, I disliked Germans. Even though I excluded Mother's relatives from my prejudice, I absolutely refused to identify with them in any way. I was Dutch and so was Mother. I wanted her to speak Dutch all the time – she spoke it flawlessly, without an accent.

I must confess that I often wished that my mother was different. I wanted her to be more ordinary, more unobtrusive and more like the mothers of my friends. I cringed when Mother came to the Lyceum in high heels, sporting the latest hat from Paris, a fashionable fur coat flung over her shoulders. I wished I had a mother who arrived on her bicycle, wearing sensible flat shoes and an Egyptian cotton raincoat belted at the waist.

When Omi wasn't competing for Mother's attention, she was a lovely grandmother whom you could tell your secrets to, and who was always generous with advice and special treats. When she came to live with us, it was she who brought me the little gold-trimmed leather book which was to become my diary. At first, I used it as a scrapbook, carefully pasting into it photos of my favourite film stars cut out of magazines. But soon I was passionately recording my daily thoughts and doings:

6 February 1939
I've had enough of pasting pictures in this album. So I've decided to begin a diary. I hope to illustrate it as well – whether I will or not is another story. I think it's a little risky to record my deepest secrets here, because you never know into whose hands this may fall some day.

Maybe it was the fact that my mother suddenly had less time for me that made me turn to my diary. Or perhaps it was because, being the youngest, I felt I wasn't always taken all that seriously by my family. At dinner, there would be animated discussions on subjects that I knew little of, and my big brothers would ignore me when I tried to say my piece. When I finally piped up, wailing, 'Not fair, *I* never get a turn!', Father would hold up his hand, and tell the boys to be quiet. Then, making a great show of looking at his watch, he would say, 'All right, Edith. You have exactly two minutes to talk. Ready – set – go!' Stammering foolishly in the unfamiliar silence, I was usually unable to remember what it was that I had wanted to say – until my time was up. In my journal, however, I could chatter away to my heart's content, leap-frogging from one thought to another with no one to answer to but myself.

24 *February 1939*
Today I finished my geometry – not too well, I think, I'm not sure though, it could be good. Tomorrow we're going to a youth concert. I'm looking forward to it. Because I'd so like to learn all about music, I mean classical music, so that I could understand it and appreciate how beautiful it is. I'd like to really be able to enjoy that kind of music. Now I enjoy the lighter kind of music. Piano – I love it. I wish I could play the piano. Jazz, too – piano jazz. I like it for a while, but then I've had enough. I have a new plan for my future. I want to be an architect, or something to do with children. I want to help sick children or poor children – give them a lovely holiday. I want to have a house in the country, and have children come for holidays. I hope in any case that some day I'll have my own house, with a good man and sweet kids. I hardly ever dare to express my feelings, in speech or here, on the page. But this kind of feeling isn't really that intimate. I mean, most girls hope for the same kind of thing. I have to study my French.

I'd better not say anything about the hockey match against Hudito – except to say we lost 5–0, just as we did on Sunday.

Within three and a half years I had filled seven notebooks, and I was hooked for life.

My father's name was David van Hessen but he was known to his friends and family as 'Dago'. His parents had agreed to let him train as an artist on condition that he learn a trade as well. The business Father went into was timber: he was the European representative of the Ritter Lumber Company of Columbus, Ohio. He used to tell us that he was happy with the choice he had made. Rather than devote his life to art (and risk us all starving in a garret), he had vowed to be a good provider for his family. He used to say, 'I'd much rather be a first-class amateur than a second-rate artist.' Art did remain an important part of his life, however. At home he was never without his sketchbook or his paints. He had converted a WC on the third floor into a darkroom for his photography; a corner of his study was his sculpture atelier. It was one of my chores to keep the clay on the revolving pedestal behind his desk moist when he was away. His work was sometimes shown in group exhibits, and business trips abroad enabled him to cultivate acquaintances and exchange ideas with artists such as Käthe Kollwitz and Paul Prött.

It was on one of those business trips that he had met Mother, at a friend's wedding. Mother claimed she knew immediately that this tall handsome Dutchman was the man she was going to marry, but it took a second chance meeting in the streets of Heidelberg, some months later, to convince Father. He said it was the best decision he had ever made in all his life, to take for his bride the striking, dark-haired young woman, who lit up his formerly taciturn and stolidly middle-class life with colour and breeziness and passion. After the war they set up house in Amsterdam, and in 1920 my brother Guus was born. Two years later they moved to The Hague, where my other brother, Jules, arrived in 1923, followed by me, the only girl, in 1925.

My mother had a good voice and played the piano, my father played the violin and the guitar, and together they would sing sentimental ballads like two lovebirds, to our great delight. Father enjoyed reading poetry to us, or stories by his favourite authors, O'Henry and Mark Twain. My brothers and I were encouraged to be creative. Guus loved to paint windmills and often went on landscape-painting expeditions with Father, armed with his own little paintbox and easel. Jules repaired boats and made all sorts of vehicles using salvaged materials. (One day, intending to take my dolls for a walk, I discovered the wheels of my doll's pram missing. They turned up on one of Jules's ever more ingenious go-karts.) I tried my hand at everything, from the accordion to cartooning.

Even though it was said that it had taken some adjusting for my aunts on Father's side to adapt to their exuberant and decisive sister-in-law, I remember warm and harmonious family gatherings. Birthdays and wedding anniversaries, especially, were celebrated in grand style. There were always poems, speeches and tributes composed in flowery language, expressions of love and admiration, as well as the occasional joke or sly caricature sketched by Father.

When Mother turned forty, Father gave her a gramophone record on which each of us in turn read a poem, or made a little speech. It included a song composed by Father, which ended, '. . . and when we are very old and we have come to the end of our life I hope I'll be able to say to you, "Come, Hilde, come, we haven't lived in vain . . ."'

*

In 1939 Father was fifty-eight; I had three years of secondary school left, and my brothers had not yet started university. As he did not have a pension, Father did not see himself retiring until his three children had finished their studies. Whenever I saw a worried look on his face, I imagined it was all because of me. I was growing so rapidly that I was constantly in need of new clothes or new shoes. I told Mother that I'd do anything to make him cheerful again – I'd even return the new skirt we had bought, or wear my old shoes even though they pinched. But Mother reassured me that there were other things bothering him, and my rapid growth had nothing to do with it.

I was thirteen and my head was full of school, friends and fun. My friends were everything to me, and I had many of them. So did Jules. I was a little shy around my brothers' friends, because they were older than me. That did not stop me, however, from tagging along whenever they would let me. One of Jules's schoolmates was Loet Velmans, whom I remembered from summers at the beach when we were little, chiefly as the most agile and tanned of all the children swinging on the monkey-bars.

I was in the second year of secondary school when I first met Miep Fernandes at the Lyceum's rowing-club. She was as immediately convinced as I that we would be friends for life. Miep was older than me and in the third year; she and her family had recently returned to Holland from the Dutch East Indies, where her father, an ophthalmologist in the army, had been stationed. The family was originally from the West Indies.* After hearing each other's stories and meeting each other's families, Miep and I decided that our parents were sure to become friends if we introduced them to each other,

---

* The eldest daughter had the unusual name Guyanina, Nina for short – after Dutch Guyana, where she was born.

because they had so much in common. Sure enough, our parents did become good friends, and other friendships developed, most notably between my cousin Paul and Miep's older sister Nina.

Miep and I decided to write a comic opera together, a cabaret-like farce that took place in a beauty salon, complete with funny lyrics set to popular melodies. It was to be performed by our drama club at a special theatre-and-music evening before the entire school.

But another piece of excitement eclipsed even the writing of a comic opera: we were about to take possession of a new sailing-boat! We named it *De Doolaard*, which means 'wanderer' and was the name of a popular Dutch author.* Every chance we got, my brothers and I would be down at the dockyard admiring our new boat. We were all avid sailors, including Father. Summer was for swimming, rowing and sailing; winter was for skating. Politics meant nothing to me. I remember Jules sprawled on the floor, leaning on his elbows with his feet waving in the air, reading the newspaper spread in front of him. I never asked what it was all about. I was too busy to care.

A sense of foreboding hung over my life, however. Once, during dinner, the telephone rang. Father got up to take the call, and I caught Mother watching him with a worried expression. Then Father turned his back on us, bending his head and pressing it into the earpiece as if to hear better, and Mother exchanged a concerned look with Omi. I knew something was terribly wrong. But Mother reassured us, saying we shouldn't worry. We protested that we didn't want to be treated like little children. When Father put the receiver

---

* A. den Doolaard had published, in 1938, *Swastika over Europe*, in which he warned that war with Germany was inevitable. It was a message no one wanted to hear, and the book was not a commercial success.

down, I implored him to tell us what happened. Father finally said, 'My brother – your uncle Leo – just died.'

'Oh, is that all?' I thought, relieved. I had been expecting to hear something much worse, although I didn't know exactly what.

In my diary, I wrote down a poem of which I was rather proud:

Thunderstorm
Threatening clouds hang over the ocean
Swarming with birds, flying along in motion
Here it comes
Here it comes
It's dark over all the world.
The people take cover
In terror at this malice unfurled.
Now it bursts,
A flash of fire,
A thundering knell
Rolls over houses, fields and woods,
Lights up the trees down in the dell.
Then, at the climax of its force,
Explodes again, unleashes the worst
A bang! and then a creaking,
A blinding ball of fire streaking
And then suddenly all is still,
It's over,
And everyone who can thank God, will.
– BY EDITH VAN HESSEN, 18 JUNE 1939

By September 1939, it was impossible not to notice that scary things were happening. After Germany had invaded Poland, I couldn't help hearing Adolf Hitler ranting and raving whenever the news was on the radio, nor could I help seeing his moustached face in the paper. I knew that Hitler hated

Jews. Britain and France declared war on Germany, and Holland's military forces were mobilized – just in case.

This held an unexpectedly exciting consequence for us children: my parents decided, after much debate, that it would be a good idea to build a bomb shelter. The shelter was built at the back of the garden, where it took up an unreasonably large piece of the lawn. Our gardener covered it with grass sod, and Mother planted daffodils all round it. We furnished the interior with empty crates that served as tables and benches, with a few pillows thrown in to soften the austere atmosphere. To make it more homely still, books, ashtrays and a torch kept company with the gas masks Father had gone out to buy, and soon our shelter was the most popular spot in the neighbourhood. We formed secret societies and played poker by candlelight, and sometimes my brother Jules and his girl-friends played other mysterious games in there, in which I was not invited to participate.

Near the shelter grew a young pear tree that was Father's favourite. In the spring, when the tree was in bloom, Father would call me out to the garden to show me the beauty of the white petals with their rosy cheeks and long dusted stamens poking out of their centres. The stamens made me think of Betty Boop's eyelashes! This, he would explain, is where the fruit starts growing, '. . . and when they are ripe, Eetje,* we'll have our *own* pears for breakfast!'

Every morning before going to the office, Father walked down the steps of the terrace to study the plantings, touching a branch here, a stem there, as if to implore them to function abundantly. Every morning we received a report on the state of the pear tree. There were six, seven, eight young pears forming on the tree. 'Don't play ball in the garden,' we were told. 'Let's not spoil the harvest . . .'

* One of my nicknames.

Then, one morning, Father brought in three small, unripe pears, fallen too soon from their branches and half eaten by the birds. The next day two other pears were found lying on the ground. 'Why don't we just pick the others now?' I asked. 'No good, darling, they aren't ripe yet,' was the reply. I couldn't wait – the suspense was killing me.

Finally came the big day. There was only one pear left. We all trooped down to the pear tree, where Father, following Mother's directions, picked the fruit. In his hand was the biggest, fattest pear I had ever seen. He carried the precious harvest into the dining room, the rest of us following solemnly in procession. With his silver fruit knife Father cut into the pear.

Flawless as it was on the outside, the pear was rotten to the core inside. Father looked up at us with a rueful grin. 'We have waited too long, I guess . . .'

2

The Passports

Father had taken the precaution of obtaining entrance visas to the United States for the family. This had not been difficult, since he was the president of a branch of an American firm. Mr Ritter, the head of the parent company in Ohio, had offered to sponsor us and provided the US consulate in Rotterdam with an affidavit. There was one hitch, however. Omi was not included. As a former German national, currently 'stateless', Omi did not fit into the immigration quotas. The US was flooded with applications from German Jews, and had closed its doors to them for now. Omi would have to stay behind. Upon arrival in the USA, my parents were assured, they could certainly apply for a refugee visa for her, which would be processed on its own merits. But for Mother, it was impossible to leave without Omi. And Father, unable to bring himself to force the issue, kept procrastinating. He felt it would be heartless to leave the old lady behind. Also, his children did not make it any easier for him: Jules and I were unwilling to give up our sailing-boat, our happy life and our friends. We did not see why we should uproot ourselves.

It was decided, however, that Guus, the oldest, should go. He was nineteen, and about to be called up into the army. Guus had always been a fragile child. Chronic bronchitis had kept him indoors for much of his early life. He had been having treatment with a Dr Zuyling – a specialist who believed that the boy's condition required complete rest, healthy mountain air and a hefty diet. At the age of eight, Guus had been sent to a sanatorium in Saanen, Switzerland, where he had been fattened up and cured of his bronchitis. But he returned a chubby, clumsy boy, who preferred the company of adults to that of other children. He was not as athletic as Jules and myself, and did not participate much in our games. Jules was a sports enthusiast, darkly handsome, outgoing and very popular with the girls. Guus was a lone tinkerer, always messing around with radios and amplifiers in his room, and I think my parents worried about him.

Coming home from a lecture on 'The inferiority complex and the quest for perfection' by Alfred Adler, the German psychologist, Mother announced that she'd had a flash of insight: Guus had been over-protected, and it was necessary for him to 'learn to stand on his own two feet'. Even though he was just months away from sitting for his finals, it was decided he should go to America at once.

17 February 1940
Guus, when he receives his visa, is going to go to America, to Columbus, to work in the forests, in Father's timber company. He'll get a year's deferment of his military service. I hope that he'll make it far, so that we can all be proud of each other and happy. Happiness, that really is the greatest factor in one's life. I've understood it now, that it's not just about getting, it's also about giving. To make others happy, that's what makes you happy. I'm usually pretty catty to my brothers, but in truth we like each other a lot.

I've been eating so much lately that people are astonished to see me always chewing on something, whether I'm lying down or sitting up. I think I'll end up in the circus as the fattest woman in the world, the kind you're allowed to prick with a pin to assure yourself that it's no trick – what an attractive prospect! At least I'll make a decent living. Actually, what I really want to do is to become a doctor. Study medicine. I decided this a few months ago. I hope I'll make it. To heal people, not to have to go into business, always grubbing after money.They say, leave that aspect to your husband, but I don't really agree, because it's important to know how to do something yourself in times of need; who knows what will happen, you don't want to be left empty-handed. I've started practising. I'm training myself to be able to stand the sight of blood, and to be brave, and if there's been an accident, I'm going to make myself go and watch . . .

On 10 March 1940 we all piled into Father's old Chevrolet to take Guus to Rotterdam, where was docked the ship that would take him to America. I felt great admiration for my big brother, who suddenly seemed so grown-up, so strong and courageous, embarked as he was on a big adventure, far away from home. Father and Mother hugged him as if they would never let him go. There were tears, brave smiles, and feigned bravado. To my embarrassment, Mother couldn't stop waving, even when Guus disappeared into the crowd on deck, and I was sure he couldn't see us any more.

17 March 1940
We've had lots of news from Guus. Cards and letters and telegrams. The first telegrams were full of 'stop', but it got too expensive, so Guus has now stopped stopping his sentences with 'stop'. We just got a telegram, 'Arrived in America well and healthy as can be.' Wonderful for Father and Mother to know for sure that he's arrived safe and sound, in the arms of family and friends.

In my Easter holiday I took a three-day bike trip with ten schoolmates through the east of Holland, staying in youth hostels. I filled many pages of my diary with a blow-by-blow account of the trip, complete with anecdotes about holding hands with various boys, the menus of our simple meals, the friendships and the capers I was embroiled in. In contrast, my reporting on what was happening in the world and the state of Father's health – he had been suffering from a problem with his larynx – was understated to the extreme.

20 April 1940
Lots has happened.

(1) Politics: Denmark is now Germany, and we wake up every morning with the question, 'Are we still Dutch?'

(2) I've been going out a lot. Loads of fun.

(3) Father has just had his third operation (his surgeon was Dr Fernandes, Miep's uncle) and now his voice sounds much better.

And then there was the party, last night, at Kitty's. Twelve boys and twelve girls. We played games, we danced and ate a lot. Jan de S. took me home, with Anneke and Riet in tow. We were all wearing evening dresses. *Très chic*. Of course I spilled some orangeade on my dress!

3

The Invasion

10 May 1940. 4.30 a.m.
I was just woken up by a great banging outside. With my
groggy head, all I wanted to do at first was to go back to
sleep. But then I realized that the sounds I was hearing were
. . . gunshots!

Everyone is awake. The neighbours are all standing at
their windows, you can see exactly what kind of pyjamas
or nighties they have on. All of a sudden I feel so close to
them.

Masses of aeroplanes have been flying overhead. The
anti-aircraft guns parked on the field behind our house are
shooting like mad into the sky – bullets that give off light.
What a racket! As if all hell has broken loose! Never in my
life have I seen or heard anything like it. And so near by,
too! Right behind our house. The bullets were just whistling
right over our roof and past my window. There are heavy
dark smoke clouds and little grey puffs, like bubbles, everywhere you look. Meanwhile, you can see the sun come up.
A beautiful day. The gardens are bursting with spring
flowers. What's going to come of all this? Is this us against
them, or us against us? Whatever it is . . . it's certainly not
the way things are supposed to be. What's the future got
in store for us? Don't know. But things have calmed down,
for now. It's quiet again. I'm going to try to get a little
more sleep.

5.45 a.m.
This is it. It's for real. We have to get dressed. We just saw
a plane get shot down! It's the Germans. I have to get up!

Father, Mother and Jules had all gathered in my room just
as a plane came crashing down near our house. Its tail was
on fire. We guessed it landed in the Haagse Bos, the woodland
park where I often hung out with my friends. I could see
two parachutes in the air, with little human figures dangling
beneath them like toys. For a moment we all just stood there,
mesmerized. Then Father cried, 'It's the Germans! Everybody
get dressed at once!' I felt dizzy with excitement and dread.
It was like being in a film.

The neighbours had all come out into the street, in their
dressing-gowns and slippers, and Father went out to join
them. I had never seen any adults (besides my own parents)
in night clothes before. It really must be serious. I pulled on
some clothes and went downstairs. My diary and my pencil
came with me. I had a mission – to report events as they
happened.

9.40 a.m.
We're at war with Germany. They're fighting at the borders.
There are non-stop bulletins on the radio. Practically
nobody is going to school today. I just heard over the radio
that all the schools are closed. I was outside a few minutes
ago, with my friend Jackie B. W., who lives on the corner,
when the shooting started again. We had to run to an
air-raid shelter. Terrible! The world is upside down. But
the English and the French will come and help us, you'll
see. Courage!

It was Father's words I was echoing. 'Courage,' he said.
'Let's hope for the best. That's all we can do.' We were glued
to the radio, listening to bulletins from the front. Our army

was putting up a valiant fight in the east and south of the country. The government ordered all citizens to tape black paper over their windows, in preparation for a black-out when night fell. I felt shaky, more excited than afraid, as if I was on the verge of taking an important exam, or standing on the highest diving board at the pool. I felt inexplicably proud to be Dutch, and I was determined to help in any way I could.

9 p.m.
We're all hanging round the living room biting our nails. Everything's dark outside. Black paper taped to everyone's windows. It really feels like the war is being fought right here in our own back yard. Masses of Germans have been shot dead. Spies. Pretending to be Dutch, wearing Dutch army uniforms. Right around the corner, they dropped a bomb on the barracks. At least sixty of our soldiers dead. Poor boys! And it's all happening so close by. It's incredible. I can't believe this is really happening.

Jules has joined the Fire Brigade, he keeps having to run off somewhere whenever the sirens go off. This morning, when I was outside, I had to make a run for an air-raid shelter. It's quiet now. The Dutch are putting up a brave fight. We'll just have to be brave, too, and stay calm!

For the next three days, we hovered anxiously round the radio, and tried to remain calm. We took every rumour as gospel. My favourite cousin, Paul van Hessen, who was ten years older than me and had been mobilized into the army, stopped by our house in his handsome uniform to give us reassuring 'insider' information. We ventured out to get supplies, and to gape at the barracks around the corner, a portion of which had been reduced to a heap of smouldering rubble. There were military checkpoints all over the city. Paul told us that if you were stopped by the soldiers, they'd ask you to say the password 'Scheveningen' – the name of the nearby harbour town. If you couldn't pronounce the Dutch 'sch' sound, you'd be arrested as a spy. Everyone knew that no German, or any other foreigner, could imitate that particular sequence of impossibly guttural consonants. I proudly practised saying Scheveningen, to myself. No one would take *me* for a spy, I was sure.

14 May – morning

Mother's birthday. We're doing nothing special to celebrate, only lunch. Because the Germans have already occupied half of the Netherlands. Our Queen, the Princess, the Prince and their children have landed in England. The Germans have crossed the Moerdijk.* What's to become of us now, now that the Queen has given up? Paul was here yesterday, he is fairly confident. Well, who knows. But we probably won't be able to keep it up much longer. Our passports are still at the consulate in Rotterdam. Well, at least the Germans are getting a whipping. There's rioting going on, in the cities. Snipers – traitors – shooting from the rooftops. Everybody is very brave. The soldiers and the people, both. How long?

14 May – night

We have been very brave. The soldiers and the people. But – all for nothing. The cabinet has fled to England too. Today, at 12.30, we went out – Mother, Father, Jules and I. The dining table was set for the birthday lunch. But Father said we had to go and get our food ration cards first, at the Town Hall. It was impossibly crowded. The queue was way out into the street. We could see we'd never make it to the front of the queue, even if we stayed there all day. Suddenly, the sirens started blaring. Off to the shelter! When it was over, everyone scrambled back, and

---

* An important bridge over the River Waal, bisecting the country.

Mother managed to procure a place at the head of the queue. It was our turn in no time at all. What a lucky break. On the way home we had to take cover three times. The last alarm lasted one and a half hours. We were all starving by that time, of course. At five p.m. we finally had our lunch!

Later Paul dropped by again. He was pretty cheerful. (All this time we could hear the guns shooting at German planes high up in the sky.) Then we had another visitor, one of Paul's army buddies, he was also in great spirits, full of courage and hope. Well, that made us feel much better, naturally. Suddenly we noticed all the neighbours standing outside on the pavement. Of course we all troop outside to join them . . . and . . . what do we hear? It's just come over the radio: Holland has CAPITULATED!! Given up! Except for the Fortress Zeeland.

I can't possibly describe how deeply this news has shocked everyone. Everybody (practically) is in despair. Paul sad and down – his hope all gone. He has gone to surrender his weapon.

We are German now. The Netherlands belongs to Germany. We had to give ourselves up, in the end, because they bombed Rotterdam so badly that they say there's not a single house left standing, practically, and not a soul left alive. The city has been razed to the ground. In this ghastly five-day war, about 40,000* young men have been killed. Poor mothers, poor widows and orphans! They don't even have any way of knowing what's happened to their child or their husband.

I pray to God that our whole family is safe, and will remain so. Tomorrow they're coming to occupy The Hague. Everyone is desperate.

* The actual number was 4,000.

We had missed our chance to make it to America. Our passports, with their precious visas, had gone up in smoke along with the US Consulate and the city of Rotterdam. That night, standing in silence at the window of Jules's bedroom, which faced south, we could see Rotterdam's blood-red glow – a gory background for the hundreds of little black balloons drifting down that were the German paratroopers coming to occupy our town.

4

Dick van Swaay

For me, the only noticeable change in those early days of the German occupation was that I had more household chores to do. Mother had to let Jannie, our maid, go – the first of a series of economies my parents made in case of bad times ahead. Other than that, we didn't panic. I had seen my parents shake their heads when, the day of the surrender, some Jewish friends had stopped by to say goodbye, on their way to the harbour at Scheveningen. They were leaving, they said; they would try to get out on a boat headed for England. By the next day, however, they were home again, disappointed and frustrated. They told us that there had been total chaos at the docks, with thousands of people, Jews and Gentiles, running in all directions. As far as we knew, nobody had succeeded in getting out that day. And now it was too late.

The German troops made their presence felt when they entered The Hague, goose-stepping impressively down our streets, belting out marching songs. They didn't look all that different from the Dutch soldiers we had waved to and cheered on just a few days earlier – except for the swastikas around their arms and their noisy black boots. The Germans wanted to be friendly. They whistled and winked at the girls, and tried to start conversations with us. But they got the cold-shoulder treatment. We tried to pretend they just weren't there.

19 May 1940

Things aren't that bad, really. The past few days seem like an angry dream. Everything is just as before. Tomorrow we're going back to school. My poor head isn't up to it right now. I've forgotten everything. Jannie is leaving. We have to save. The weather's beautiful. It's still light out. We had to put our clocks forward by one hour and forty minutes. I'm going to sleep.

One or two boys didn't return to school. We figured that they had found a way to join the army that had been fighting to hold off the Germans in the southern province of Zeeland. Jules came home reporting that his classmate Loet Velmans had vanished, with his cousin Dick Speyer (a boy I used to play with when I was little), and their parents. No one seemed to know what had become of them.

The news was bleak. Menno ter Braak, a leading literary critic and author much admired by my parents, committed suicide. Others followed suit. Father received a call that his cousin Mary, who had an important job in the government and lived round the corner from us, had been found dead in her kitchen with the oven-gas on. Aunt Mary, who had never married, had been a regular, if not particularly memorable, visitor at our house. My parents were pretty shaken by this news. As for me, I just couldn't understand how some grown-ups could have so little hope, so little faith in the future, when there were still so many good and beautiful things left in the world – things I seemed to be seeing as if for the first time.

2 June 1940

Evening. A peaceful calm has settled around me. Dusk. The sky is a soft blue, threaded with wisps of pink. Across the street I see the silhouettes of trees in which blackbirds are still chirping. The sound of light footsteps in the distance. Voices. Inside, my little alarm clock is ticking loudly. High in the sky hangs a star, right across from my window. It's there every evening and it shines more brightly than any other star that I can see from here. I just stand here and watch, every night. It's so beautiful . . .

We were sure that the enemy would be beaten back quickly. They would never make it across France's Maginot Line, said cousin Paul. Never! The French defence line was just too strong. But before we knew it Belgium was overrun, and Paris fell on 14 June.

14 June
We had a lovely evening. Father recited Heine. So did Mother, Jules and I. Nina and Paul came. We all played music. It was wonderful.

Paris is now occupied by the Germans. But here things have calmed down. Not so in the rest of the world . . . !

Mother complained of not feeling well. Father said it was nerves and anxiety. Guiltily, I thought it was probably my fault, because I was so selfishly preoccupied by my own life.

4 July 1940
(I'm at school. Mr Hilbers is correcting papers, and there's nothing for us to do.) I turned fifteen yesterday. The best birthday ever. The morning started off pretty well. I got a voucher for a three-speed bike, Fl. 12.50 cash, a pair of gorgeous shoes, and lots of flowers and sweets, etc. Also a beautiful bouquet of tiger lilies from the florist, with a card, 'From a secret admirer', and another anonymous bunch of sweet-peas, I have no idea who sent them. Anyway . . . A big birthday lunch, with visitors, and then, in the evening, more visitors – a party! And then the best surprise of all – an overseas telegram from Guus, in rhyme, no less. Mother and Father were so happy. We had tea and three birthday cakes baked by Mother and Omi, and twenty-four pastries,

and ice-cream. At nine p.m. we all went into the living room. Mother sang Schubert, Miep's grandfather showed us some magic tricks, my friend Dolf played Schumann's *Papillon* on the piano, we tried to have a séance, Jules and I recited a poem together – I stood behind him, with his arms hidden and my arms gesturing, it was very funny. The others performed sketches, etc. Then Father gave us his own hysterical version of a poem by Schiller, mixing up all the lines; I laughed so hard tears ran down my cheeks. I couldn't get to sleep before one, I was so excited. Pity, though, that Mother wasn't feeling well, and had to work so hard to clean up from the party and of course I wasn't much help. I've been shamefully spoiled, everyone was so wonderful, I never expected to have such an incredible birthday in these difficult times. What a shame Mother's birthday had to fall on the day of Holland's capitulation. I feel so bad for her.

I haven't done a thing in class all morning except write in my diary. Now it's Mr Koolman's turn, he's rattling on about something, I don't need to listen, we've already spent four lessons on this subject. Hannie, who's sitting right in front of me, just turned round to tell me that if you write in a diary that means that you're 'stuck on yourself'. Nonsense! But I'd better go so I can pay attention to the last five minutes of Mr Koolman's brand of 'Rationalism'.

The summer flew by. We spent a lot of time on our sailing-boat. Jules had a summer job in a factory that made vacuum cleaners, but it didn't last long: his hand was caught in one of the machines, and two of his fingers were badly injured. It took most of the summer to heal, and it meant he did not have to help me with the dishes. My grandmother was ill in hospital; I visited her faithfully. I was in the girls' rowing team and spent hours training on the canals near the Lyceum's boat-house. I have to admit that this was partly because I was very taken with a sixth-former named Dick van Swaay, who was our rowing coach. That summer we spent almost every day on the water, sailing and rowing and teasing each other. I basked in this older boy's attentions. The only problem was that one of my girlfriends, Noeke, liked him too. In September, Dick left to go to university, and I went back to school.

6 September 1940
I've started the year very poorly. Can't do anything right. Messy and disorganized. Oh well.

All foreigners* have to leave The Hague. There are very few parts of Holland where they are now allowed to live. Most places are off limits to them. Omi got a notice too. But she's in the hospital. Let's hope that she'll be allowed to stay with us. Something fishy is going on and I don't like it.

There are five girls and twelve boys in my class this year. This afternoon we had an election for class representative. Dick R. was chosen as class president, and I was elected vice-president. Nobody said we had to have a boy and a girl, it just turned out that way. I'm very excited and pleased.

I was also chosen to be secretary of the drama and music club, complained about my maths homework, worked on the comic opera, and spent hours training for the rowing-club races in the pouring rain – the weather was cold and nasty that autumn. Dick van Swaay, though he was now a first-year at Delft University, had stayed on as our rowing coach. He had promised to whip us into shape for the inter-schools races in November. On our afternoons off, every Wednesday and Saturday, my friends and I would meet at the boat-house in

---

* By 'foreigners' the Nazis meant Jewish refugees, mainly from Germany, but also some from other parts of Eastern Europe.

Leidschendam, a good hour's bicycle ride from school. It was when Dick was there that we were at our best – bright and witty, the atmosphere sparkling and light. That was because all the girls wanted Dick to like them.

Noeke and I were his 'special little' friends. We knew that he was fond of us. After our training sessions, we'd hang around the boat-house until it was almost dark, playing poker, mucking about, collapsing into hysterical laughter. Sometimes I was sure he had special feelings for me; at other times I got jealous of the attention Noeke was getting.

One day after a hilarious training session, we all descended on the village of Leidschendam in search of a milkshake or an ice-cream. Dick linked his arm through mine. A shiver went through me. I was in seventh heaven, walking on air. Surely this was the declaration I had been waiting for. I wanted our intimate walk to go on for ever. But then came Noeke's voice, calling me. 'What?' I said giddily, and leaned back to hear her. She'd been walking on the other side of Dick. Then I noticed that Dick was walking arm-in-arm with Noeke as well!

Another day we decided to go to the Cineac after rowing practice. Going to the pictures wasn't much fun any more, since the cinemas now showed nothing but German films. But at the Cineac, which was devoted to newsreels and current events, they were showing a short film about the 1936 Berlin Olympics.

Finally, after sitting through endless news footage of 'glorious German victories', there was what we had come for: the finals of the women's freestyle swimming. And there she was, our Rietje Mastenbroek, Holland's fastest female swimmer, collecting her gold medal. The newsreel showed the Dutch flag being raised slowly while the Dutch national anthem was played.

Next to me in the dark of the cinema, I felt Dick rising

deliberately to his feet. He stood at attention, saluting the flag. My friends and I gasped. There he was, a lone, solemn silhouette outlined starkly against the lighted screen. Around us people were shuffling nervously in their seats. Like them, I was too scared to follow his example. But I was certain that I was not the only one in that darkened cinema wishing I had the guts to join in Dick's simple act of resistance.

As soon as the music stopped, we got up and slunk out of the cinema as quickly and as unobtrusively as we could. 'Dick! What did you do that for! Don't you realize what could happen to you . . . ?' we whispered once we were round the corner.

'So? I don't give a damn,' he said defiantly before we split up and rode silently to our separate blacked-out homes.

That was one of the last times I saw Dick van Swaay. It was only many years later that I learned that while he was playing around with us, Dick was already active in the Resistance. He had successfully arranged the escape to England of a number of fellow students. He himself was not so lucky. When things became too hot for him in Holland, in September 1941, he set out in a canoe equipped with a sail and headed for England. He and his companion were caught and sent to an SS prison in Rotterdam. Dick managed to escape, however, and set out to sea again, in another canoe, on 14 November 1941. His body was later washed ashore at Noordwijk. He was twenty years old.

5

Skating

I tried to help out at home, but I frequently got into trouble. I could never make the deadlines my parents set for me, I often came home late and was occasionally grounded. I remember my parents accusing me of being so busy with my own concerns that I neglected my duties at home. But they never stayed mad at me for long.

13 October 1940
Yesterday was the Day of Atonement. I fasted from seven p.m. Friday until 7.15 p.m. Saturday. I didn't drink any water and ate nothing. Walked to the synagogue with Mother in the afternoon. At dinner we fell on our food like starving wolves. I really felt good about it. To have made this sacrifice, for God and myself. It makes me strong. We've been receiving lots of mail from Guus. A treat. He's such a wonderful boy. It's taken all this time for his brother and sister to start realizing that. Father, Mother and Omi are crazy about him.

Omi is all better. Had dinner with us. Regal in her flowing robe and high heels. She's an angel. She's been able to help Mother again with the housework. I'm too lazy. I'm really hopeless.

Our wireless radios were confiscated. It was illegal to listen to the BBC. There remained only the four German-controlled stations that we could listen to on the radio-diffusion box wired into the phone lines. There was no real news, only propaganda and reports about the German armed forces' advances and victories. But I didn't care as long as I could still listen to my favourite tunes – 'Mood Indigo', 'The Tiger Rag', 'Georgia on My Mind' and my all-time favourite, 'Stardust', played by the Ramblers, a popular Dutch jazz ensemble. Everybody said the war couldn't last much longer; by Christmas we'd be free again.

The partying continued uninterrupted. Jules was supposed to be studying hard, because it was his last year of school; his final exams were coming up in the spring. But he was easily distracted by his busy social life. Several girls, including Miep, confided in me that they were in love with my brother. He said he liked them all, but was not interested in having a serious relationship with any one girl.

We kept hearing about Jewish acquaintances who were getting fired from their jobs. The *Moffen* (the insulting name we called the Germans behind their backs) had been busy issuing new decrees. There were to be no new appointments or promotions of Jews in the public service. All businesses owned by Jews, including Father's, had to be registered with the authorities. All government employees were required to sign a declaration that they were (or were not) of Aryan descent. I reported in my diary that the university students in Delft and Leiden had gone on strike in protest. Miep's sister Nina and my cousin Dolf van Hessen had participated, as had Dick van Swaay. Next, the Dutch churches sent out a joint letter protesting about the singling out of Jewish citizens. Within a week of the protests, all Jewish government employees were dismissed from their posts.

On 5 December, the feast of St Nicolaas (a secular holiday on which presents are exchanged in Holland), Mother had packed our gifts inside an elaborate life-sized Neville Chamberlain doll she had made. I went to a St Nicolaas party the next day, and rebuffed a boy who tried to kiss me.

Jan de S. took me home. He insisted. When we reached the lane round the corner, he put his arm around me. I let him, because it was either that or bumping into him or into the walls. We turned into my street. At the corner, in front of Jackie's house, he suddenly tried to kiss me. I didn't like that at all. Yuck. I pulled my head back and said, 'Hey Jan, stop it!' He let go and said, 'Well, bye, I'm going home,' and I quickly said, 'Aren't you supposed to escort me to my door?' So he did, and then all we talked about was school.

I confessed to my diary that several boys liked me a lot, and I was pretty pleased with myself. On 20 December, to celebrate the holidays, there was a tea dance at my school.

First I danced with Dicky P.; he's a little weak – he's just too good and too sweet. He lets people walk all over him. Then we lit the candles, and I danced with Walter V. Then with Ernst. Then Jan K. asked me to dance. We didn't say too much. I mentioned the mistletoe. Then he asked me if I'd give him permission to make use of it. I said, 'Well, I'd rather you didn't.' He asked me to dance several times after that, we even danced the last dance together. People say he is NSB.* But I think he's nice. Good-looking. At the end of the party, when everyone had gone home, my girlfriends were indignant about Jan being NSB and then asking me to dance and all that, but – well, what can you do? Anyway I don't believe it, otherwise why should he pick me to dance with, of all people.

My parents did their best not to let their anxiety show too much. On New Year's Eve Father put on his dinner jacket, Mother was resplendent in her red sequinned evening gown and we had another of our wonderful family celebrations.

---

* i.e. a member of the Dutch National Socialist Party; Dutch Nazi.

First we played cards. For cents. This is how it is for Mother and me: whenever we're winning we're having a great time, but if we start losing – watch out! Suddenly Omi came downstairs, in her pink dressing-gown, a pink bow in her hair and a basket on her arm. She launched into an aria from an Italian opera. We fell out of our chairs laughing, she was so funny. She was really excited. In the middle of her song she suddenly moaned, '*Ach, lach doch nicht so, Hilde* . . .' (Don't laugh so, Hilde . . .) Then we had punch. My first glass of punch ever. Then we all had to make a speech. Mother had some sweet and moving words for us; then it was my turn, a little shy and silly, I can't make speeches, but Jules did well, and Paul too, he is like a brother, he really belongs here, and of course Father made a magnificent speech. I just sat there and listened and thought – I am so very lucky to have such parents and such a family. Then I said to myself, 'Happiness isn't just parties and boys and going out; happiness is here, with the people to whom I belong . . .'

Nineteen forty-one! Will this year bring us something better than 1940 has? Will the war finally be over? Nobody knows. My wishes for the new year are: health, happiness and many more New Year's Eves. Peace. Guus back home with us. Omi with us for many more years, and all of us together – for now and for ever. And now it's 2.30, and my second journal is full. I end the old year and this diary together with the hope that this old Afrikaans saying will come true: '*Alles sal reg kom!*' (Everything will turn out all right.)

It was a very cold winter, all the more noticeable because heating fuel was rationed. I spent many a night cuddled up to my trusty hot-water bottle. But I didn't mind because the skating that year was fantastic. We often made excursions along the frozen canals – you could skate all the way to Leiden or other nearby towns. Vendors had set up stalls on the ice, offering hot pea soup or hot chocolate. When we girls got tired and started lagging behind, we'd find a broomstick or rod of some sort to hold on to and the boys would pull us along. We laughed a lot and covered many miles that way. One very cold day Jules and his friends took part in the 'Four Lakes Skating Tour'. To finish in this ninety-kilometre race was considered quite an accomplishment.

Because of the blackout, the street-lamps were not lit at night, and we had to grope our way home with torches. But we discovered that when the moon was full, you didn't need a torch. The moon lit the way and revealed our shadows like long spiky ghosts. Before the war, with street-lighting and the houses themselves all lit up, I never realized how bright the moon could be. There was a little park near our house with a pond where we went skating in the moonlight with our friends.

I put on my skates at home. It's just like in the winter sport, in the Alps – you step out of your house into the snow. The moon shone, the snow glittered. On the way to the pond I slipped a few times, but finally got there, wearing Father's duffle-coat. There were lots of Jules's friends, his new girlfriend too. I attempted to figure-skate. That is to say, I attempted to *attempt* to figure-skate. I managed not to make too much of a fool of myself. Two boys had brought their guitars. People hummed and whistled along. It wasn't cold at all. When you looked around, you saw the ice, the moon, the trees, young people milling around. At times all you saw was the glowing tips of cigarettes. All of this, with the music, made me think of summer evenings on the lake. It was such fun. I skated with Jules and then some other boys. Then Herbert F. asked me. He's a terrific skater. We danced a waltz. Then the fourteen-step, which I once learned at the Skating Club, but I didn't remember it too well. Still, I began to get a little more confident, then a little too cocksure, with the result that I found myself sprawled on my backside on the ice. Never mind. Another boy had brought a gramophone, and set it up on the ice. Then we all watched Herbert figure-skate. It's awesome, the way that boy can skate – foxtrot, waltz, tango, anything. When he got tired he stretched out in the snow on his back. Suddenly Father arrived to take us home. I knew he was mad. I just left and went with him, not saying a word. Jules called after us that he had to take Nina home. On the way home I got a terrific scolding for staying out too late and not putting away my bicycle, etc. I hobbled after Father as best I could, on my skates. When we got home I was still pretty much in the doghouse, but at least I acted as a lightning-conductor for the drubbing Jules would have received. It was too bad that Father got so mad. But he forgave us in the end, so that the evening wasn't totally spoiled for Mother and Omi.

The month of January was taken up with rehearsals for our comic opera, *Chez Antoine*, and preparations for the drama club's big night. My grades suffered, but I wasn't too concerned about that, although I was sorry to miss out on some of the skating and sledging.

1 February 1941
We spent the entire morning in the auditorium, building the sets. Meanwhile the Ice Festival was in full swing. To tell you the truth I was miffed that I couldn't go, but you have to make sacrifices for your club. When you're older I guess you have to make sacrifices too. So this is a mini-training for the future. The future, when I'm older . . . I wonder, how far away is that?

The dress rehearsal wasn't too great. Mr Busch kept talking about Edith's Salon de Beauté. The set is fabulous. It really looks like a beauty salon. Pots of cream, little bottles filled with coloured water, posters and advertisements, and a wonderful huge saw for the wart-removal scene. Later someone even brought in a standing hair-drier. But it was frustrating – Loulou wouldn't learn her lines. She kept forgetting the last words: 'Madam, you look *extraordinary*.' Every time she forgot 'extraordinary', the audience would howl with laughter.

Ran home to get changed, then back to school for the big performance. At first the auditorium looked sort of empty. But then it began to fill up. There were quite a number of teachers. The headmaster was a pain, getting in the way as usual, but what can you do? I was the one who had to introduce the teachers during the interval. The programme mentioned our names, Edith van Hessen and Miep Fernandes, as authors of the piece *Chez Antoine*; it was the last thing on the programme. It went pretty well, except that I took the drier away too soon, so that when Margo, who had been sitting under it, yelled that her hair was on fire it didn't make any sense. Oh well, most people didn't seem to notice. At the end, when it was time for Loulou's last line, all the kids who had been at the dress rehearsal shouted out from the back of the room, 'Madam, you look *extraordinary*!' which was pretty funny. I loved it. When it was over Mr Busch climbed on to the stage and said something about 'this wonderful play and this very successful afternoon' and talked about the two students who had written and directed it, and then he mentioned our names. More applause. Everyone came up to us to congratulate us and tell us how wonderful it had been, including the teachers. Then we took our flowers and went home. It was hard to get my make-up off and now I'm dead tired.

6

Jews Not Welcome Here

It was announced that every citizen was to be issued with a new identity card; passports were worthless from now on. A bold letter 'J' was to be stamped on it if you were Jewish. 'Not a good omen,' sighed Mother. Father tried to reassure her. 'If that's all the Nazis intend to do to us, it's nothing. Don't let it get to you, darling. After all, here in Holland they'll never get away with some of the things they have done in Germany. Don't forget – this is Holland!'

6 February 1941
More snow. Everything's white. Sounds are muffled. People are slipping, sliding and falling all over the place. Today I wasn't in the best of moods. A little disappointed in myself. I went to visit Miep, who didn't go to school because she wasn't well. A friend of theirs has been arrested. We're all supposed to register, we can't postpone it any longer, and I guess we'll get a 'J' stamped on our papers. Anyway. Whatever happens, happens. I don't want to think about it too much. Letter from Guus, dated December. He's so happy there, he's turning into a real American. Only he misses us, of course, but he says he thinks the country is even more beautiful and wonderful than our own lovely little country. Then it must be pretty special! He describes all sorts of domestic appliances, butter, tinned goods, advertisements, the bright lights, etc. and we meanwhile sitting

here in the dark, simply drooling over his descriptions of the good life over there. . .

Miep's parents decided that they would take the risk of not registering as Jews. Since they had both been born on Surinam in the West Indies, their names were not in the Dutch birth registry, and therefore there was no official record that they had Jewish grandparents. As for my family, we obediently registered as was required. Once we got our new papers, I told everyone that I was proud of that 'J' on my ID card. My parents encouraged us to hold our heads high, and not be ashamed of who we were.

We read in the newspaper that, after a riot in Amsterdam's Jewish quarter in which a Nazi sympathizer had been killed, 400 young Jews had been dragged from their homes in a *razzia* and rounded up for transportation to Mauthausen, a concentration camp in Germany.

11 February 1941
'Seize the day,' says Mother. But I'm worried. At home everyone is so optimistic, but others are pessimistic. Many people are hanging around aimlessly in the streets, out of work. There are riots and demonstrations. It doesn't bode well for us. *Enfin.* Let's hope that '*Alles sal reg kom*' – soon! Actually, I'm an idiot to grumble on like this. I'm still enjoying my life as much as I can.

A general protest strike, organized by the Communists, followed the riots. It lasted three days before the Germans managed to break it.* But all this was happening in Amsterdam, that big, confusing city that was only an hour's train ride from our town but seemed half a world away. It was

---

* According to the historian Louis de Jong, the 25 February strike may have been 'the first and only anti-pogrom strike in human history'.

Amsterdam that now had a crowded Jewish quarter, with the largest concentration of Jews in the country, including both poor people and recent immigrants who had been forced to move there by the Germans. We felt that nothing like that would ever happen in civilized, elegant The Hague, although we were affected just as much as our Amsterdam brethren by snowballing new decrees. Jewish doctors, dentists and other professionals were no longer permitted to treat or perform services for Gentiles. When Father had to go somewhere on business, he had to take the train – we had had to hand in our Chevrolet.

The effect of all this on me was that I suddenly became more aware of my Jewish identity. Up until this point, my religion had never seemed an important part of who I was. Apart from the Jewish holidays, there was not much emphasis on religious observance in my family. Omi was the exception – there was a dog-eared prayer-book beside her bed and she was always lighting *jahrzeit* candles to commemorate her beloved ones' deaths. At school my friends were Protestant, Jewish, or Catholic – it had never seemed to matter very much. But now I was curious to find out what this being Jewish was all about. I accompanied Jules to a meeting of a Zionist youth group, Gideon, and was invited to join, which I took as quite an honour, since I was the youngest one there. I was impressed by the heated intellectual discussions, and sometimes tried to join in. I don't have a very clear recollection of what these discussions were about; they seemed to focus on pure theory and philosophy. I don't think I paid all that much attention. To be perfectly honest, what *I* liked best about the youth group was the boys . . .

11 February 1941
I'm so glad I got into Gideon. I feel very much at home there. It's a tremendous honour, to be picked as a member

when I'm only fifteen. They are all much older. I really belong in another group, there are other clubs for my age group, but they really wanted me in this one. It's so much fun. Lots of laughs (I hope it will always be that way). What I just wrote may sound conceited, but it does everyone good sometimes to feel wanted and liked. Some days I feel this more, some days less. But let me declare here, in case of inferiority complexes to come, that there are some people who like me, and some people who think I'm nice. So there. What the others think of me, I don't know. But at least I don't have any enemies – none that I'm aware of, at any rate. I want to have friendships, always, and love everyone, and only see the goodness in things and in people. To get back to what I was talking about, Bob was very attentive to me, which I of course appreciated immensely. (I realize that on every page of this *Sturm und Drang* diary a different boy's name is mentioned. Well, what's the point of being a girl otherwise?)

I did a lot of soul-searching, and attributed my adolescent mood swings to horrible defects in my character, especially when I detected in myself what I perceived as immoderate conceit.

12 February 1941
I've been in such a weird mood all day. At school I couldn't stop talking, acted the clown, insulted my classmates, had to apologize; then, at home, I chattered on at the dinner table, jumping from one subject to another, usually unimportant things about myself. I realize that I had a silly grin on my face all day. Was singing to myself on my bike. Went to Miep's house after dinner. I noticed (the moon was dark) that I was standing there on her doorstep – grinning. Was laughing when I went in. Silly all evening. Kept going into hysterical giggles – sort of fun, but also tiring. Draining. I

am much too conceited these days and am always talking
about myself. I feel so unnatural today. Hope I'll be normal
again tomorrow. I'd better get some sleep so that Morpheus
can help me back on track.

I did take time out from worrying about myself to worry
about Mother, who was having recurrent gall-bladder attacks.

2 March 1941
We were sitting drinking tea and reading our books when
Mother suddenly doubled over. It was terrible. Father and
I running up and down the stairs with hot towels. Poor
Mamsy. She is so brave, and she suffered so. Omi kept
insisting on getting out of bed, asking whether there was
anything she could do. In spite of everything we had to
laugh when Omi came into the room, gingerly, her hand
on her own poor sick head, proffering her bottle of *eau de
Cologne*. The lame helping the blind . . .

My mother's suffering was more worrying to me than the
war. But there was more to it than simply concern or sympathy.
I think that in my mind, Mother's gall-bladder and even my
own little aches and pains were a test, a way of proving how
strong we could be in facing hardships in an uncertain (and
never talked about) future.

6/7 March 1941
After entertaining Paul and Nina, who had come over, I
went to bed. Father came up, and turned off my light. I
promised I wouldn't turn it on again. There I was in the
dark, having all these thoughts. Suddenly I felt happy, in
spite of my period pains – I decided it was good to feel
pain, because I wanted to harden myself, to make something
of myself, to become a better person. I want to be tough,
to teach myself to be cheerful whatever happens. I got up
and went downstairs because I had this urge to tell Mother

and Father that I realized I was grateful for my cramps, when suddenly I heard Mother moaning. I knew what that meant – it wasn't anything new. Another gall-bladder attack. Oh, it's so dreadful when Mother gets one of these attacks. And she's so brave, but the pain is so terrible. And all we can do is stand there and watch. And supply her with steaming hot towels. We'd like to do more but Mother has to bear this alone. They sent me back to bed. I was ashamed of my own silly little cramps that had made me so happy that I had decided to tell Mother and Father about them! In the meantime my cramps had vanished. I went and sat on the stairs to listen. Gave myself a scolding for being insensitive and self-centred, I don't know why. Suddenly as I was sitting there I had this inspiration: I'm going to write a book – not an ordinary girl's story but something much deeper. I know how it will begin, too: 'No, young reader, this book has nothing to do with romance . . .'

Suddenly Father stepped out into the hall. I tried to hide, but he saw me and told me not to worry, everything was fine. I slunk back upstairs. I sat on my bed brushing my hair. Footsteps on the stairs . . . It was Father, to see if I was all right. Mother was feeling better. He stayed and talked a while. Then he kissed me good night, and told me to turn off the light. I must confess to my great shame that as soon as he'd gone I turned it on again in order to write all this down. One funny thing Father told me: in order to spare Omi any worry, when he went to borrow the hot-water bottle from her he said that it was for him. So then later on Omi comes into the bathroom with a bottle of cognac for Father, because she is worried about poor Father being so cold!

Next door all is quiet. As usual, Jules has slept through the whole thing. At least he'll be rested tomorrow. Not me!

*

I was determined to improve my character. To that end, I asked Mother to teach me some of her favourite aphorisms.

7 March 1941
Tonight I asked Mother to repeat some of the wise sayings that are good to know if you want to have a good life. E.g. from Schopenhauer, etc.: 'He who believes in goodness will gain goodness.'

And: 'Trouble is the scale on which the true worth of friendship is weighed.'

And I just found this one in my pocket diary: 'Look at the sun, then your shadow will fall behind you.'

The war seemed far away. Our bomb shelter in the garden remained unused. We were occasionally woken up by sirens, or even the sound of bombs falling; I would turn over in bed and go back to sleep. My parents often acted tense and distracted. But still I tried to remain oblivious to these signs, and to make myself turn a blind eye to the more ominous news.

15 March 1941
Yes, it's true that there's a lot to cope with these days. The situation isn't exactly rosy. Another air-raid siren a short while ago. But that's nothing serious.

What I failed to mention in my diary was that neighbours had reported hearing gun salvos two days earlier, and the newspapers had announced that fifteen 'traitors' had been executed by firing squad in a field not far from our house. They were members of an early anti-Nazi resistance group that called itself the 'Geuzen' (named after a rebellion against the Spanish occupation of Holland in the sixteenth century). Several hundred Geuzen had been arrested at the beginning of the winter, and the show trial took place in The Hague.*

I was unaware of most of this at the time. I was trying to hang on as long as possible to the picture I had of the world as a good and safe place.

15 March 1941. 11.30 p.m.
I'm sitting on the window-sill in Jules's room, writing by the light of the moon . . . a full moon . . . I can't see a thing, can't see what I'm writing . . . It's very quiet outside . . . Once in a while the silence is broken by the droning of an aeroplane . . . Shadows are falling into the room, on to my hands and on to the paper. I'm hanging halfway out of the window. Below me I can see the garden, brightly lit. The drops suspended from the leaves glitter in the moonlight and make everything look like crystal. The trees are drawn in black against the greyish sky. I can hear Father and Mother talking in their room right below me. Everybody is enjoying this beautiful evening . . . Everything is peaceful and lovely. How can it be that just down the street a horrible war is going on?

Oh, how I wish I could go to sleep right here on the window-sill. But if I do that, I'm likely to fall into the garden. No, I'll go and find my own little bed, and try to banish all thoughts of balmy days and lovely evenings and moonlight from my head!

In April we received our report-cards, which put me in a good mood, because I had done rather well. My composition teacher had liked one of my essays so much he had read it aloud to

---

* After the war we learned that the Geuzen had been unspeakably tortured. The man who had originally betrayed them was one of those shot near our house. He went to his death pleading for his comrades' forgiveness. Of those who were not executed, 175 were sent to Buchenwald concentration camp.

another class. My art teacher had praised a 'dramatic drawing' I had been working on and said he found it 'moving'. I had called it *Souls Attempting to Escape from Hell*, and it showed lugubrious shadowy figures clambering out of a pit. Even my chemistry teacher, Mr Kaptein, had a compliment for me – although chemistry was my weakest subject, and the compliment a back-handed one.

5 April 1941
I got a $6\frac{1}{2}$ for chemistry – not bad, considering. When Mr Kaptein gave me back my paper, he said: 'Well, Edith, I've got to say that when I correct papers, I usually do it sitting in an easy chair by the fireplace, in my dressing-gown, smoking my pipe. But when I get to your paper, I suddenly start feeling uncomfortable, and wish that I was dressed properly. Then I stroke my chin, to see if I need a shave, and all this because you use such fancy, *erudite* language . . .' Well, the whole class cracked up, of course . . .

At Miep's yesterday I played, or tried to play, the piano for about three hours! After dinner I went home, and then there was this scene:

Grandmother, mother and child sit around the table. It is the hour between day and night. The room is veiled in semi-darkness. The child reads her essay to the grandmother. Then the mother takes a candle from the mantel, places it on the table and begins to tell a story. A story about something that had made a big impression on her when she was young. After that she reads a lovely poem, about a woman who learns to forgive. On the table there is a basket of flowers that casts wonderful shadows over the tablecloth . . .

Despite my disappointment in some people who seemed to be finding it necessary to hide their Jewishness, or others who didn't see any harm in working for the enemy, I thought it better not to be overly critical. Paul de R., a boy who used to skate with us and was always coming by the house to use Jules's blade-sharpener, told us he had signed up for *Arbeidsdienst* – a volunteer work brigade to support the German war effort. I had briefly had a crush on him earlier in the year, as we'd had a lot of fun skating together, and I was sure that his eagerness to sharpen his skates had something to do with me. But when I discovered that he was pro-German, I decided I didn't like him any more. I had nothing to say to him when I next saw him. Still, when he stopped by one last time before going off to work in Germany, I wrote:

> *11 April 1941*
> It made me feel good, to think that even though he is in the *Arbeidsdienst*, he still likes to come here. I have, in spite of everything, a little soft spot in my heart for him. Silly, isn't it? Where others would have antipathy, I have sympathy. Never mind.*

It was the Easter holidays. As we had done the previous year, a group of classmates and I took off on a challenging three-day, 236-kilometre bike trip, often in the pouring rain, with difficult head winds. It so happened that I was the only one of the group who was Jewish. At night we stayed in youth hostels. When I got home, I felt triumphant, having fought the elements and pushed myself to my physical limit. There was just one part of the experience that was a little hard to digest, however.

> *20 April 1941*
> It really gives you a sense of satisfaction, to know you can

---

* Some months later, we heard that Paul de R. had ended up in Russia. Like many of the Dutch boys in the *Arbeidsdienst*, he never came back.

do it, that you really achieved something. I'm sitting on my bed, with a sunburnt face and aching knees. Apart from that, everything is normal . . . except my state of mind. I need cheering up a little. You've got to admit it's a little upsetting when you enter a small village, and you see a sign: JEWS ARE NOT WELCOME HERE. There was a little café in Wilnis that we walked into on the first day. Nice people. They had a sign too but they kept it hidden in a cupboard. They showed it to us. It said JEWS NOT WELCOME. They'd refused to hang it up. We saw similar signs in other villages. Oh well.

I had until the end of the week to get used to the idea: a decree was published that cafés as well as cinemas were now off-limits to Jews in my home town of The Hague. Jewish musicians employed in state-sponsored orchestras were dismissed from their jobs. At the last youth concert at which Jews were allowed to play, I took the thundering accolades for the Jewish concert master of The Hague's Symphony Orchestra as a kind of personal vindication.

4 May 1941
It was the last concert for Sam Swaab, the concert master. Beautiful music – Beethoven's eighth, and his fourth piano concerto, with Nelly Wagenaar, soloist. Willem Andriessen was the conductor. When Sam Swaab walked out on to the podium, there was tumultuous applause. Again after the symphony. Then at the end, when Andriessen leaned forward to shake Swaab's hand . . . the audience went wild. Me too. People were stamping their feet. The hall was shaking. I was very moved.

7

A Heart Full of Love

The first anniversary of the German invasion came just as I was beginning to realize that this war might not turn out to be as short as I had been hoping.

10 May 1941
One year ago today they invaded our country . . .
　　At school it was great. Deathly silence. Hardly anyone was talking or laughing. At break everybody kept their mouth shut. You could hear the shuffling of about 400 feet but not a word. Outside all you heard was hollow footsteps, sombre and deadly, and when we went back inside it was like a funeral service.

It was around this time that I became interested in a new boy, Adrie Verhulst, who was to become my boyfriend and whose family was to be instrumental in my survival. Adrie, a.k.a. 'Aat', was another of Jules's many friends. I found out from Jules one day that Adrie liked me, after he had been at our house to discuss boat-building with Father and Jules. I was downstairs in the living room trying to do my homework, but the conversation was so distracting that I had to put my fingers in my ears in order to concentrate on my geography. Soon afterwards Adrie asked me to be his date at a party given by a former girlfriend.

The ex-girlfriend's name was Loes, and she confided in me that she was half-Jewish, but did not want the others to know.

She was very mature for her age, and was breaking up with Adrie because, even though he was a year older, she considered him too young for her. The party was for Loes's seventeenth birthday, but she told everyone she was eighteen. Her basement had been decorated with Japanese lanterns and festive lights. I puffed on a cigarette – my first – and Adrie and I drank May wine out of the same glass. Somebody turned out the lights. We danced to 'Stardust' and 'Dancing Cheek to Cheek', and then Adrie kissed me.

But you can't just write that down, 'then he kissed me'. Your first kiss. That's something you keep for ever, inside.

Adrie took me home, his hand around my waist as we pedalled our bikes side by side down the deserted streets, and he kissed me again. At home, Father and Mother were still awake and Jules and I sat on their bed and told them all about the party. Then Jules and I went to my room to compare notes, arguing about which of us had had a better time.

The next day my joy was all gone. It was a day filled with terrible news. First I heard that in the night a bomb had fallen on a house in the same block where the party had been. All the windows in Loes's house were shattered. What a sad end to the most wonderful night of my life! Then we read in the paper that public swimming-pools, beaches, parks and racetracks were now off-limits to Jews. I didn't care too much about the races, but not to be allowed to go to the beach . . . ! It was ghastly. Finally, my friend Alice Cohen came to tell me that the Germans had come to her house to hand her family a final notice: the house was being requisitioned. I had always been rather envious of Alice's house, which was bigger and grander than ours, on the corner plot of our street. Now I was glad I lived in a terraced house that didn't stand out, in the middle of the block. The Cohens had to be out by the end of the month, and were warned not to take anything with them except clothes and personal belongings. The furniture was to stay behind. It was being confiscated in the name of the Führer.

When Alice left, Miep and I dragged ourselves outside to work on our trigonometry homework behind the bomb shelter.

> The bomb shelter is coming in very handy these days. I use it to lean against, as a backrest. Suddenly we heard a loud commotion, roaring and shooting, and then we see this plane come racing right over our house, very low, at tremendous speed. It turns out to be . . . the Brits! Everybody starts cheering and yelling. In broad daylight! More shooting, and a short while later . . . air-raid sirens. We just stayed right where we were in the garden. Then we heard somebody leaning on the doorbell. And guess who it was? . . . Adrie and a couple of friends. Seeking 'shelter'. They joined us in the garden. It was fun. We had a great time.

One evening after doing the dishes, feeling industrious, I put on overalls, knotted a scarf around my head, and marched down to the air-raid shelter with a broom and bucket. I would show everybody what a wonderful housekeeper I was. I found crushed corpses of large beetles on the ground, long-legged spiders scurrying up the walls, mouldy potatoes with long purple shoots, yellowing newspapers and a single battered old shoe. The stale air and fluttering spider webs gave me the creeps. I had wanted to make it homely and nice, so that we could use it for Jules's graduation party. But the more I swept, the more dust I created. The earthen floor and concrete walls were not good candidates for a scrubbing. There were still ants crawling everywhere. It remained what it was – a damp and filthy pit. A grave! Finally I gave up. Like the war, the shelter could not be made clean and nice, no matter how hard I tried.

*

We defied the new laws against bathing by meeting our friends after school on a deserted stretch of beach far from the popular public beaches. We called it 'The Green House' – after the green cabin perched above the sand that was the only sign of habitation. The walk through the sandy dunes was hot and tiring (because of an unexploded bomb, the paved path to the beach was closed), and by the time we got there it was usually getting late and I often wasn't in the mood any more. But into the waves I'd go nevertheless, grimly determined. After all, my non-Jewish friends had gone out of their way to come here to show their solidarity; I owed it to them to enjoy myself.

Mother's health was not improving. The gall-bladder attacks came on more often and she sometimes had to take morphine for the pain. I wished I could help ease her suffering and blamed myself for adding to her worries; but in my breezy way I couldn't help minimizing any problems, so that when Mother had to enter a nursing-home to try to recover her mental and physical strength, I accepted her going as a perfectly wonderful solution.

8 May 1941
At four o'clock, after a moving farewell from Omi, I set off with Mamke – I, proudly, carrying her suitcase as far as the tram. It's so wonderful for her that she can finally get some rest, the dear. She has to get better. The house in Wassenaar is called 'The Ivy', a beautiful villa. A nurse is the head of it, and there are all sorts of people there who are in need of rest. Mams has a beautiful room on the first floor and she really is in good hands. I saw lots of good Dutch books in the bookcase. Omi and I miss her already . . .

I found a substitute for my now frequently bedridden mother in Omi. It was three years since my grandmother had moved into our house, time for us to get used to one another and for her Dutch and my German to improve. One lovely spring night, when Father was away and Mother was in the nursing-home, Omi and I slept together in my parents' big double bed. With the doors to the balcony wide open and the curtains drawn back to let in the moonlight, we talked and giggled until well after midnight. I was beginning to appreciate this gentle soul with the creamy white hair for whom a dab of *eau de Cologne* was the ultimate panacea, and whose tremulous sighs were a reminder of things that had happened long ago and that were suddenly beginning to seem interesting to me. We retained our new closeness even after Mother returned.

> *31 May 1941*
> Well, yes indeed! I am very, very happy at the moment. Had a wonderful evening. Father and Mother went out visiting. Omi, Jules and I stayed home. Omi and I knelt on the living-room window-seat, gazing out at the dusk falling. Omi told me things about the past. All the old memories. About Mother and Father: how they found each other. Then Jules joined us. We listened to records and drank tea. Omi made a big fuss over the tea tray, she prepared everything beautifully. Then we sat in the dusk with the lights off. I kept playing 'Stardust' over and over. I love that record! Very sentimental; just the right note for the hour of twilight. I listened to it with my eyes closed. I also told Omi all about the friends I go round with these days – Paul, Adrie, Dicky, Dick, Wim, etc. (That seems conceited, that 'etcetera', but it's true: there seem to be a lot of boys in my life these days.) But I'm so happy today. I have a heart full of love, a poet might say, or something.

Adrie was constantly coming round. By eight o'clock on week nights, my watchful father would come out into the hall where we stood smooching and say, firmly, that it was time for Adrie to go home. Still, both Father and Mother said that he was a nice boy. I told my diary proudly that they knew that they could 'trust us'. But I was worried that other people would start thinking I was 'that sort of girl' – either 'boy crazy' or a 'party girl'.

14 June 1941

I spent hours in front of the mirror fussing with my hair. Finally I put the finishing touch to my *toilette*. The entire family had to come and make reassuring noises about my looks. (What a despicably vain, frivolous creature I am!) Aat picked me up at 7.45. Because of the rain I had wrapped myself in dozens of scarves, to Aat's great amusement, with the result that poor Aat had to carry at least a third of them around in his pockets. Well! The party at Boy's house: we danced round the dining-room table, I danced with Adrie the entire night, except for one dance with Boy. I think I'm beginning to fall a little bit in love. Well, I guess that's to be expected. We danced the last dance in the dark: leading to some very happy memories. I won't say more, except that it was a lot of fun. Still, I hope I'm not getting to be one of those party types. At 11.30 the party broke up. I swathed myself in my scarves once more and the two of us trotted home, arm in arm. We couldn't get the hula music of the last dance out of our heads, and we pictured ourselves in Hawaii, far from the war, basking in the moonlight.*

Jules passed his final exams, and we had a party for forty-five friends in the garden to celebrate. Adrie, swearing me to secrecy, confided that he was thinking of 'disappearing' (i.e. going underground or fleeing to join the Allied forces). This bothered me terribly, especially since I suspected that if he was plotting something like this, Jules was probably involved as well. I walked around worrying about it for days. I couldn't

---

* It was six months later that the Japanese bombed Pearl Harbor.

tell my parents – that would have been betraying a confidence – but I did discuss it with my Hebrew tutor.

1 July 1941
Adrie wants to leave. I think it's a terrible idea. Mrs Rabinkow told me that I should speak up and tell him what I think. So I did, today. Told him exactly where I stood. Told him to consider the grief that his mother will have if he suddenly disappears, and his father, and everyone. I just suddenly let it all out. He said he understood completely, and said he would talk it over with his father. I was so relieved!

My sixteenth birthday came. At school I was the centre of attention – all my friends as well as people I hardly knew came to shake my hand. As usual, I was terribly spoiled. My parents gave me what they knew I had been hoping for – a piano. A baby grand, no less. I received a new tennis outfit, and there were dozens of other gifts from my friends. There had also been a letter tucked under my plate at breakfast. It was from Adrie, and in it he told me he had decided not to leave. That was the best gift of all.

8

Banishment

4 *August 1941*
That's that. My fourth diary is full. Now for my fifth one.
I wonder if this is the book in which I'll be able to report
Peace or Victory for our side. Everyone is optimistic. Per-
haps everything will turn out all right. Just about the entire
world is now involved in the war. Britain–Russia–Canada.
Against Germany – Italy – and all the occupied countries.
Japan against Indochina. What is to become of this world?
Oh well . . .

We got a letter from Guus, for Dad's sixtieth birthday.
Beautiful letter. Proud of my oldest brother! He writes that a
friend of Mother's has committed suicide in a concentration
camp in France. Mother was very upset. How desperate
you must have to be, to take your own life. Things must
have seemed very bleak, her daughter in America, her son in
a training camp in Canada, husband also in a concentration
camp, she herself a prisoner and a diabetic to boot. Poor
woman . . .

The big issue between my parents and me was my lack of
sensitivity to what was going on around me. They tried to
impress on me a sense of responsibility, and I would fly off
the handle.

8 August 1941

I am a horrible, unpleasant child. Not a nice daughter. A nasty, cold, selfish, spoiled girl who only acts happy and sweet when she can run around with boys, etc.

That's according to my father and mother.

I am not at all a good daughter; Esther V. and I don't know how many other girls are much nicer and more polite than I am and know how to please their parents, and even that saleswoman in the Bijenkorf* who always helps Mother has more reason to be proud of her daughter than Mam . . .

So – I am impossible.

That's what I had to listen to tonight. Apparently I acted sullen and distracted in front of the visitors. I thought I had been trying very hard not to be self-centred, and yet it seems I am too selfish. Well, then I must be a horrible child, if they say so. No, I think it would be better if I just left home so that I wouldn't be a burden to my parents and disappoint them all the time.

We never stayed mad for long. Mother and I had kissed and made up by the next day, just in time for our big film project. As a surprise for Father on his sixtieth birthday, we were making a film called *A bicycle tour through Father's life*. All the relatives showed up for the occasion; I had to sleep on the floor, having given up my bed to my cousin Renée. Even one of my Catholic uncles, Uncle Alfred, showed up. I called him my 'sugar uncle' because he always brought me treats. He took Renée and me to Rotterdam the next day to show us the aftermath of the bombardment of May 1940. I think he felt sorry for us. (My grandfather's brother had converted to Catholicism in the nineteenth century. When my

---

* A large department store.

great-uncle was gravely ill, he made a vow to the Sisters who nursed him in the Roman Catholic hospital in Groningen. If the nuns prayed for him, he told them, and he recovered, he would convert. He did get better, and he kept his promise. Most of his descendants, including Uncle Alfred, survived the war.)

Father's birthday was a typical van Hessen celebration, although the adults seemed more emotional than they had been at family gatherings in the past.

13 August 1941
Yesterday afternoon at lunch there was some serious speech-making going on. Uncle Louis sat at the head of the table; Uncle Herman sat next to me. Lovely uncles. Uncle Louis was the barometer for all of us. If a speech or a poem was sufficiently moving, then Uncle Louis would start weeping buckets. Everyone had a speech or a poem. Father too. Aunt Marie was the last to go; she soon dissolved in tears but bravely kept going till the end. Uncle Louis sobbed along. Jules made a funny speech, in his inimitable way. A poem from me. I think they liked it, at least I noticed that even I managed to bring a tear to Uncle Louis's eye.

Father had been working hard on a terracotta bust of Mother he was sculpting. We all thought it was the best thing he'd ever done. He had captured her softness and her radiant, yet pensive smile. One evening in August, the sculptor Albert Termote, who was Father's teacher, came to dinner. I tried to make a good impression: Father had told me that Mr Termote was quite famous. Solemnly we trooped into Father's study to hear the master's evaluation. Termote rubbed his chin. He turned the revolving pedestal. He cleared his throat. Mother's bust was declared finished; a success. It was ready to be cast in bronze. We all sighed with relief and beamed with pride.

That same evening we learned of further draconian restrictions on the Jewish population.

21 August 1941
Alice came over. She is very depressed and looks awful. Times are pretty bad. Jews are not allowed to keep more than a thousand guilders of their income. Apparently that's a pretty low blow. And other measures too. But I don't care. As long as Jules isn't picked up and sent away, as long as we can stay here in our cosy house, I can stand anything, and I hope I'll be able to help others. Poor Alice, I don't think she's got much guts. She gets downhearted so quickly. Oh well, I guess most people are depressed these days. But I want to be strong! I want to come out of this war tough and unbeaten. And if we're not allowed to go to school any more, well then I'll just keep on working, and learning things, and getting wiser!

At first it was just a rumour, but soon the decree was published officially in the Jewish newspaper *Het Joodsche Weekblad*:* Jewish children were no longer allowed to attend public or private schools. My friends were indignant. I told everyone I couldn't care less. I didn't need any sympathy. I'd survive even this, good sport that I was.

Suddenly we discovered who was Jewish and who was not. We had never been aware of any differences in our crowd. Some kids went to church or celebrated Christmas, some were 'nothing', and some went to synagogue on the high holydays. Of my best friends, Alice, Miep, Dolf and Dicky were Jewish;

* *The Jewish Weekly* – published by the Jewish Council under the supervision of the occupying forces.

most of the others, including Adrie, were not. It was something we had never paid much attention to before.

24 August 1941
And what do you know! This evening it was in the newspaper: we're not allowed to go to school any more. You see.

I took this news over to Dolf's house. Maud was there. She, terribly indignant. Thought it was too bad and said that all the fun crowd would now be gone from school, and only the boring people left. Anyway, we came up with a terrific idea for an American party to mark the end of the holidays and we decided not to let the new situation bother us. Later went over to Margo's house for her birthday. Everyone was so sympathetic about our not being allowed to return to school. The Dutch are a wonderful people! Home by eleven . . . the Fernandes were just leaving, they'd come to console us. Not necessary. We'll survive just fine. '*Alles sal reg kom*' and that's why I refuse to worry and am going to think about something really lovely until I fall asleep . . .

Over the summer I had been given an extra assignment in chemistry, my weakest subject. Now I received a message from my chemistry teacher, Mr Kaptein, that he wanted to see my work. Kaptein was the teacher who used to tease me about the pedantically precocious language I often employed to cover up my ignorance. Since I wasn't allowed in school any more, I was to go to his house.

31 August 1941
August is over. It is September. Yesterday was our Queen's birthday. Today the streets were littered with all sorts of flyers, garbage saying things like: 'Yankee, Englishman, Chinaman and Bolshevik/Dance to the music of the Jewish

clique.' Those last words printed thickly, in red. There were dozens of them plastered all over the street lantern right in front of our house. Down the street, on the other lanterns, there were only a few.

After much searching and asking for directions, I finally found Kaptein's house. Was welcomed warmly by Mrs K. Mr K. took me into his study to talk about everything. He felt so bad for me. He showed me pictures of the baby, and Mrs K. brought the baby upstairs to show me. He is such a cute child – he has changed a lot since the last time I saw him. Mrs K. is a lovely person. Then Kaptein looked over my assignment. I didn't have to answer any questions, he just filled in the blanks in my book and tried to explain stuff to me. So I don't think he noticed the lacunae in my poor brain. Before I knew it, it was time for me to go. Mr K. shook my hand and said, 'Well, Edith, I wish you all the best and I hope that you'll be back with us at the Lyceum very, very soon.' He held on to my hand for a long time. He was very moved when he said it. I was pretty touched myself, looked him straight in the eye and said softly, 'I hope so too, sir.' Mr Kaptein had tears in his eyes. He helped me into my coat and I thanked him for everything. He held the door open for me and said again, 'Goodbye, Edith, and keep your chin up, do you hear?' 'Goodbye, sir,' I said, and I ran. I'll never forget this afternoon. The sympathy and kindness they showed me . . .

Showing everyone how happy and optimistic I was turned out to be hard work. I reported to my diary that I could hardly eat from the effort. Miep was returning to the Lyceum for her final year, as was my friend Dolf, a gifted pianist whose family was of Jewish origin but who, like the Fernandes family, had found a way to hide that fact from the Germans. I boasted that I was delighted that I was still officially on holiday, while my poor friends had to go back to school. For their part they complained that I was *so* lucky, because the weather was beautiful and the water was warm.

2 September 1941
This morning I had to return some books to school. When I inquired I was told it was best if I didn't show my face at school . . . so I just gave my books to Margo, to hand them in for me. Funny feeling, that, not to be allowed to ride through that gate that you've cycled through every day for four years, not to be allowed to set foot in the building that you've grown fond of, whose auditorium you've often worked hard at decorating for special occasions, to make it nice for others in your spare time . . . *Enfin*, this too shall pass.

My rowing-club decided to organize a big send-off for those members who now had to leave school. To be off the rowing team, not to be allowed to show my face at the boat-house where I had spent so many happy afternoons – that was pretty hard. My friends thought a final outing would be a nice way to mark the break-up of our team. But Mr Quast, the coach, called the trip off because he considered it 'too risky'. My friends protested. I just shrugged. I was getting a little embarrassed, frankly, at all the sympathy and attention I was getting.

5 September 1941
Yesterday was their first day of school. Miep came by with a box of chocolates. Very sweet of her to want to console me, but I really don't need it, she's the one who needs consolation, because it's awkward for her to be at school now, with everyone asking her how come she's still there. I'm so lucky. Everyone is so nice and commiserating. It's as if I'm still at school; I know everything that's happening there, I'm keeping up with my schoolwork and I'm not a

bit bored. Girls keep phoning me: everyone wants to know how I am and no one has abandoned me so far . . .

At two o'clock Maud picked me up and we went to the beach. But in the dunes new signs had been posted: FORBIDDEN TO JEWS and RESTRICTED AREA, so Maud suggested, if I didn't want to go on, that we should go back and have tea at her house instead.

I was now part of a new group – my friends Hannie, Alice, and the twins, Polly and Dolly. We were the Jewish outcasts. We got together to work on the homework assignments supplied by our former classroom teacher Mr Dommisse, and took cooking lessons from a nice Jewish widow, Mrs Bakker, who taught us how to make custard and apple sauce and whose name ('baker') fitted her talents perfectly. One morning Hannie and I passed our old school just as it let out. We were immediately surrounded by schoolmates and teachers who told us how much they missed us. Even a very quiet, introverted boy named Eric who hardly ever spoke up came over to shake my hand and tell me he missed my 'moral support'.

Soon we were receiving semi-private instruction from various Jewish teachers and professors who had been dismissed from their teaching posts. My uncle Joost was our German language teacher. It was strange to have an uncle for a teacher. I called him 'Dr van Hessen', not 'Uncle Joost'. Meanwhile, Mother had been attending meetings of the Central Conference for Jewish Education – a group set up by the Jewish Council to organize a new primary and secondary school for Jewish students. Jules, who had intended to study engineering at the University of Delft, had nowhere to go either. The universities were not accepting Jewish students. He kept busy with some part-time jobs and, I suspect, clandestine activities.

Adrie marked the six-month anniversary of our friendship by giving me a bracelet that spelled out *Nederland* (Netherlands). He had left school, and was now enrolled in nautical college, training for the merchant marine. He wore his new uniform, with shiny epaulettes and a rakish cap, every chance he got. He looked very handsome in it, and I was proud of him. When I started having to miss parties and sporting events because of what we now called 'the Jewish question', he usually stayed home with me. His loyalty helped me to remain cheerfully defiant.

5 October 1941
On the way home some unpleasant police officer stopped us and gave me a ticket because of my eternally broken rear light. He wrote everything down, I had to show my 'J' identity card and produced it with a defiant flourish. Was not allowed to get on my bike again. I had to be home at eleven, so Aat lent me his bike and he took mine – a pity, because that meant he couldn't accompany me home, and there was a full moon . . .

9

The New School

On 8 October we were shown our new school for the first time. It was to be called 'The Jewish Lyceum'. It was a long bike-ride away on the other side of The Hague, in an unfamiliar neighbourhood of sombre terraced houses. The drab old building in Fisherstraat had stood empty for many years, and was run down and dirty, with an odd assortment of furniture. I didn't care, as long as I could get on with the serious business at hand. It was my senior year; final exams were coming up in the spring. It was to be a year of cramming and working harder than I had ever imagined possible. Those final exams were my ticket to a university education. I was determined to succeed. I had the feeling that if I didn't make it, I might not get a second chance.

The first days at the Jewish Lyceum were a time of adjustment for all of us. Two hundred students had registered. Some of them had never known about their Jewish origin until the German occupation, and they were even more bewildered than the rest of us. Dr Bartels, a friend of Father's, was the headmaster, Alice Cohen's father was head of the chemistry department, and my uncle Joost van Hessen was to continue to teach us German. It was reassuring to see those familiar faces among the strangers who were my new teachers.

With my classmate Hannie, I paid a visit to our old form and maths teacher. Mr Dommisse had been keeping us supplied with books and assignments since the beginning of the school year. We brought him flowers and thanked him for all his help. He told us he expected us to keep in touch. He said that at the Netherlands Lyceum they had not forgotten us, and that we would remain in their thoughts always. The effect of all this kindness was that I was starting to feel a little sad. I was becoming more emotional, and sometimes burst into tears at the slightest provocation.

I was feeling a bit stressed out, which explains my outburst. They say I'm not the old cheerful Ee these days, but much more moody and impetuous.

On 12 October there were rumours of an impending *razzia*, or round-up, in The Hague just like the ones that had been taking place in Amsterdam, and this sent us all into a panic.

We got home and found everything in an uproar. At first they didn't want to tell the boys, but then they did end up telling them. It seems that they're going to start arresting Jewish boys and men here also. All our men slept somewhere else last night. Jules went to Boy's house, Father and Paul to the Fernandes'. So Miep came here and slept in my room and I was downstairs with Mother. Lucky me. Except that Mother was pretty upset. But nothing happened in the end. I remained very calm throughout.

Further travel restrictions were announced. Jewish property was being confiscated by the German government office as well as by the Dutch civilian authorities. I remained oblivious to our financial predicament, but Jules was coming up with all kinds of schemes. He placed an ad in the paper for Father's old typewriter, and at least forty people called wanting to buy it. I was amazed at Jules's business acumen. He managed to get Fl. 75 guilders for a typewriter that Father had paid Fl. 60 for twenty years before!

One day I came home and noticed that Omi's prized silver candlesticks were gone. One by one, our family heirlooms and other portable possessions were quietly disappearing, 'on loan' to friends and neighbours for safekeeping. It made what was left all the more significant. I was doing my best to capture anything that smacked of happy normalcy on paper – to fix it for ever in my mind.

17 October 1941
Downstairs we had tea, the nine of us, very cosy. Then Dolf opened the piano and began to play. First Beethoven's fourth piano concerto, then Tchaikovsky's first. Lovely. We sat in the dark. Just one candle on top of the piano lit up Dolf's hands. The flickering light illuminated Mother's sculpted bust like some sort of holy image. Next to it, above the piano, Father's charcoal portrait of his mother was lit up likewise. The candlelight darting over these two likenesses of two mothers, while the beautiful music trickled from Dolf's fingers . . . I sat there by myself, listening to the music, my brother and my best friend next to me on the couch, family members everywhere; yet I was alone. But I didn't feel lonely; quite the contrary. I felt intensely happy, so joyful and strong in the face of all the unpleasantness that may yet come.

I was settling into a routine at my new school. I had agreed to help form a new social club, and was appointed secretary.

The seniors are making plans to organize dancing during the lunch break. I'm not too excited about that. *Enfin.* But break did feel just like a large comfortable family affair. Four kids were playing bridge; the others stood around watching, or chatting; I did my sewing. It's true that at a Jewish school, it's easier to feel at home, to get to know each other, than somewhere else.

72

Miep gave me a report of the final meeting of my old music and drama club at the Netherlands Lyceum, which I could not attend.

25 October 1941
The [outcome of the] last meeting of our old club left me a little sad and disappointed. I had expected something so different. They spent most of the time going over the cash ledger. They presented me with a book by Pearl Buck as a goodbye gift. But it seems nothing special was said about me. That I wasn't singled out for thanks, for all my efforts over the years. My name was mentioned only in connection with all the others. This too I had imagined differently. But *enfin*. It's behind me now, and what I should do is remember only the happy times that I enjoyed while at school and not think of the hurt. The others can't really understand, but that's the way I feel. Even my fellow officers on the committee didn't go out of their way to thank me, even though in different times they would have done so with great gusto.

My parents, concerned for my safety, were reluctant to let me go out. But as long as my friends came round to visit me, I didn't care too much.

I was invited to a party at Jetje's this evening, but I wasn't allowed to go. And there was a meeting of Choek (youth group) too. Not allowed. Tomorrow Rosa is having a party; I'm not allowed to go to that either. Not because I'm in trouble or anything. Pap and Mam just think it's better that way and I really couldn't care less.

Being elected class representative did much to restore my self-confidence. One of the boys at my new school showered me with attentions, which was annoying because I didn't care for him much and I got teased about it by my friends. One day after school, I found a package sitting on my bike, with a note. It contained a brand-new luggage strap. The note read, 'May our friendship last as many years as this strap lasts in hours.' Irritated, I heaved my satchel on to the rack and tugged at the new rubber strap so hard that it immediately snapped. 'Well, that's that,' I thought triumphantly. When I told Adrie about it, he advised me to tell the boy the truth – that I didn't like him. In the end I told him that I considered him a friend and nothing more. He finally got the message. It turned out that I needn't have bothered, for within a few weeks he disappeared. A few months later we heard that he had turned up in Switzerland.

In December we had a very successful St Nicolaas party at our house. Jules had managed to procure a six-piece band, complete with microphone, and we had a girls' 'crooning contest'. I won with a soulful rendition of 'Music, Maestro, Please'. We danced until the early hours. I was so happy that night that I was convinced that everything was going to be all right with the world.

The next day the Japanese bombed Pearl Harbor.

12 December 1941

It's Guus's birthday today. He is twenty-one – he is now of age. The young ones leave the nest. What a melancholy thing it must be for parents, to see their young ones leave home. But this, our house, will always be here for us, a haven for us all, I'm convinced of it. Our parents have done and still do so much for us . . . ! God willing, we'll be able to repay them some day – and then some!

War has broken out between Japan, America and Britain. Our Indies are in danger. They are recruiting volunteers over there. The situation is becoming critical. I don't hold out much hope for a quick end or an early peace any more.

Everything is tense and scary. It has turned into a real world war. There isn't a single place on earth that is not involved . . .

I have never written very much about the war in my journal. That's because it has never particularly interested me, and things change so every day. But it is getting worse every day, and people's suffering keeps increasing. People are dying by the millions, it's a terrible tragedy, this war . . .

Maybe it's selfish of me, that I write so little about what goes on in the big world, and only about my own unimportant little life. But I could write volumes about it, and my theories don't belong here. Your own life always seems the most important to you, that's just the way it is. It's something you are not conscious of. I, me, that's usually the focus of one's thoughts. That is just my opinion and maybe this proves I am a terrible egoist. I hope not.

My bicycle was stolen. It was my own fault. I should not have left it outside, although there was a lock on it. I went to the police to report the theft and was amazed at the crowd assembled there. It seemed everybody was being robbed left, right and centre. One girl told me her best friend had stolen her food ration card and her clothes. A milkman complained that he had lost 80 packets of butter. I attributed all this thieving and dishonesty to desperation caused by the war. A couple of weeks later I was summoned to the station. My bicycle had been fished out of a canal by a policeman. It was all rusted, the frame was bent, and both tyres were missing. My trusty old bike! If only it could talk, so it could tell me what had happened to it!

I worried about Jules, who seemed distracted, and had stopped confiding in me. I felt that he was keeping things from me. The more distantly Jules behaved, the more needy and anxious I became.

23 December 1941
When Jules heard that I wasn't allowed to go to Hans's party, he said, out of habit, 'Edith can't go? Really? That's too bad!' But then he said that he was happy that I wasn't going, because he didn't like me any more. That was supposed to be a joke. But it hurt. That kind of joke always hurts me. Maybe I'm oversensitive. But that's the way I am. To me he has always been my best friend. But he is so strange lately. He just isn't the same old Jules any more. We used to visit each other in our rooms and talk about anything and everything. We see so little of each other now. He didn't say goodnight. So I went into his room. 'Goodnight, Jules,' I said softly. His face disappeared behind his book. 'Night.' I closed the door.

Then I went downstairs to congratulate Omi on her birthday (it was 12.05). The darling. Her only wish is that she'll still be around for my wedding.

10

Frans's Jacket

1 January 1942

Hours, days, months, years . . . yes, hours, months, weeks, days, all have passed like shadows . . .

It seems like such a short time ago that we celebrated New Year's Eve last year, when things were not yet as bad as they are now. There was still enough to eat . . . There had not been as many victims of the war. Most families were happier than they are now, and the war keeps raging, getting worse . . .

Jews are persecuted everywhere, hiding out among the population, no longer secure of their lives or their rights . . . These days, everyone who bears the burden of his four grandparents' 'crime'* has forfeited all rights to human decency.

New Year's Eve was, for us, rather subdued. Father read some Balzac out loud, there were the usual poems and speeches, and I played a little piano. But Father and Mother had not put on their fancy evening clothes, and instead of champagne we drank fruit punch with seltzer. It was the last New Year we would ever celebrate together as a family.

Even though at the beginning of the invasion we had tried to make do without a maid for a while, Mother had soon

---

* The definition of a 'Jew' was anyone whose grandparents (or at least three of them) were of Jewish blood.

hired a new housekeeper. Greta had been a wonderful help, especially during the times Mother was ill. Now we learned that Greta too would have to go, because from the first of January, Gentiles were not allowed to work for Jews. A Jewish porter who had been dismissed from his job in a theatre took her place. His name was Jacques, and he had much to learn about housekeeping. It was strange to have an awkward man stumbling about the house doing the job performed so much more efficiently by Jannie or Greta. Still, I thought it was rather grand to have a 'butler'. He wore a smart red-and-white-striped jacket and certainly tried to do his best. Besides, I was happy that I didn't have to sweep or make the beds.

I really threw myself into my schoolwork that winter. It was a welcome distraction.

21 February 1942

It has been ages since I last wrote. It has been thawing, freezing, snowing, thawing, etc, etc. Now it's the big freeze again. Walking or cycling, you risk breaking your neck.

The political situation is miserable. Japan has conquered a good portion of the East Indies. Our Indies. Who would have thought it! I feel sorry for anyone whose family, father or son is over there. Horrible times we live in. In Russia things are still OK. Here in Holland at least we're all still alive. Hannie's family have been put out of their house. A bomb fell close by not too long ago. I've been getting to school late just about every day – terrible tram and bus connections. I'm still enjoying it, though. I've decided I don't want to study medicine any more, I want to study Dutch literature. I wrote an essay about a summer evening. I see very little of Aat these days. Because of the weather.

Poor neglected diary, I promise that I'll spoil you once my exams are over, I promise that then I won't be so messy and superficial. But right now I'm too tired and have too little time. Just another month and a half, and then it will all be over. And then . . . ?

I sat for the written part of my finals in April. I was nervous, yet pretty confident that I would make it. We were given a week off for last-minute revising. Our last official day of school was wild. I had written the lyrics for two songs that we sang in appreciation of our teachers. Then the entire graduating class danced the pobraise through the school, ringing the school bell, disrupting the other students, singing loudly, and offering every teacher in the building a carnation. On our own lapels we each had pinned a single happy yellow daffodil.

We didn't know that less than a month later we would all be wearing the yellow 'Jew' star in exactly the same place.

After some serious cramming, it was time for the written exams. Fighting nerves, I suddenly found religion, and prayed fervently to God every night.

After the written exams, I took a much-deserved break from studying, even though the most gruelling part was yet to come – the dreaded orals, scheduled for the beginning of July. I went sailing daily with a bunch of friends, including Jules and Adrie. Our own boat, the *Doolaard*, had been sold 'in name only' to Miep's dad, Lex Fernandes, because, as I wrote nonchalantly in my diary, 'you never know'.

But despite my relief over my exams, I could not seem to regain my equilibrium. I was acutely aware that Adrie was attractive to other girls, although he swore that I was the only one for him. There was one girl in particular, Mila, who seemed to like him a lot, and she was very pretty. Adrie was the junior champion at his tennis club, and Mila was often there with him. I couldn't go, because the club was now off-limits to Jews. Sometimes I'd wait for Adrie outside the gate, so that we could cycle home together. One day I watched through the fence as Adrie performed heroically on the court, and was congratulated by his team-mates and all the pretty girls. I felt excluded, and also lonely.

My cousin Paul bleached his hair blond, kissed Nina good-bye and, from one day to the next, was gone. I didn't know this at the time, but Paul had informed Father of his plans to escape via Belgium, France and Spain, and had asked permission to take Jules with him. After much agonizing, Father had finally said no. Entrusting him with an eighteen-year-old was too great a risk and responsibility to impose on Paul, he said.

On 2 May 1942 all Jews were ordered to wear a yellow Star of David, with the word '*Jood*' (Jew) printed on it in ugly mock-Hebraic letters. This had to be sewn on any article of clothing that was worn outside the house. I remember the instructions that came with the stars (posted around the city for all to see) specifying the exact placement of the star on the left side of the chest. There was also a poignant directive that they were to be washed first 'to prevent discoloration or shrinkage'.

4 May 1942
We're all wearing our stars. I can't stop laughing – I can't help it. It's such a hoot, this star business. You hear the most ridiculous stories, and the jokes are making the rounds faster than the rumours. The people wearing stars are greeted warmly by strangers, people take their hats off to you in the street, make all sorts of comments like 'Keep your chin up' – it's wonderful. Today apparently even a German soldier greeted Father. I had sewn mine on my scarf, you are not supposed to, but I'll just wait until someone says something about it. Everybody was incredibly nice at the

Distribution Office. Someone said to me, 'Why don't you take that silly thing off! Throw it away!' It really is a riot.

But something much worse had happened at home – something I could not laugh off. I had come home from school some days earlier to find Mother in a heap on the floor. She had been racing around the house as usual, in her high-heeled shoes, had slipped on the polished parquet floor, and passed out. She had been lying there, unable to move, for quite some time. It took a tremendous effort on my part to drag her into a chair. I then called the doctor, who came at once and together we carried her upstairs to bed. He diagnosed slight concussion and muscle injury, and ordered total bed rest.

8 May 1942
What an incredibly horrid day. Mother had been in bed for quite a few days; she was wickedly spoiled and was inundated with flowers. The doctor meanwhile had been giving her terribly painful 'massage treatments'. He wasn't sure exactly what was the matter, but a fracture . . . ? Never! OK. But today it had been ten days and she was in just as much pain as ever. Father insisted on X-rays, so the doctor was forced to change his thinking a bit. An ambulance came for her. Horrible sight, that – Mother on a stretcher. I was reassured by the thought that she wasn't *that* sick. They said they'd be back in an hour. Finally, after being away for ages, Father returned with the doctor – but without Mother! They had kept her at the hospital. The X-ray showed that there was a serious hip fracture. It will take months to heal. It was a shock to hear that. The thought of Mother being away from us all that time, and of her lying there all alone . . .

We knew that Mother was in good hands, in a good hospital, cared for by gentle nuns. Mother tried to make the best of it.

But Omi was inconsolable, and Father was deeply depressed at this enforced separation. I felt it was up to me to keep everybody's spirits up.

> But now we've all got to keep our heads above water. We'll get through this somehow. The political situation is apparently improving . . .
>
> The parade of 'stars' is dazzling. Actually, nobody pays that much attention to it any more. Most people are incredibly friendly. One lady called after me, 'Don't you pay any mind, my dear!' A little boy, this morning, piped up, 'Hello, Miss!' I don't think there will be much sailing for us any more. Everything that used to be fun is now forbidden. On the bus, when I went into town, several men offered me their seats, because of my 'star'. Another man made an unprintable comment about it and started singing 'Oranje Boven' . . .*
>
> Aat came over tonight. Was sort of down. I tried to cheer him up. We had a good talk. At least, it was a sad talk. About all sorts of depressing things. We'll just have to see how we get through all this. It's expected that by the 10th or 11th of May Mussert† will take over. I wonder what will happen then. Tenth of May is the anniversary of the invasion. Another 3,000 or so prominent citizens and officers have been arrested. As hostages, in case of a popular uprising. What next!

A young official at the Jewish Council had asked me to tutor his little sister, Bertie Keyser, a twelve-year-old who had come to live with her married brother because there was no

---

* 'Orange above', i.e. The Netherlands will win. A chant often heard at international soccer games. Orange is the Dutch national colour, based on the name of the Royal Family – the House of Orange.

† The leader of the Dutch Nazi Party.

Guus (standing) with Mother, Edith, Jules and Fifi the dog, 1938

Mother, Father and Omi on the terrace at Mildestraat, 1941

Father with Jules and Guus, 1925

Edith, 1929

Above Edith and
Jules in one of Jules's
go-karts, 1931

Left Edith after a
hockey match, 1940

Right Mother and
Father, 1938

Below Mother with
the sculpture made by
Father, 1941

Left Omi, 1941

Below Jules at his desk, 1941

Edith with Alice Cohen, 1941

Edith and Jules just before going into hiding, 1942

Above Father's sixtieth
birthday, August 1941.
Back row: Nina
Fernandes, Uncle Lex
Fernandes and Cousin
Annie Smit. Middle row:
Uncle Herman van
Hessen, Aunt Jeanette
Haas, Jetty Fernandes,
Father, Mother, Omi,
Edith, Cousin Renée van
Hessen, Aunt Map van
Hessen, Aunt Marie Smit,
Uncle Louis Smit. Front
row: Jules, Miep, Cousin
Dolf van Hessen

Left Adrie Verhulst, 1941

Noeke and Dicky at the boat-house in Leidschendam, 1940/41

Miep, Jules and Edith sailing in *De Doolaard*, 1942

Jewish school in her own hometown. My first job! I was paid Fl. 5 a week for daily tutoring. For perhaps the first time in my life, I felt the weight of responsibility for others on my shoulders.

10 May 1942
Mother's Day. I visited Mother, armed with flowers, eggs, etc. She is going to be operated on next week. Omi is not supposed to know. I am going to visit her every day. I don't have time for any schoolwork. Have to help around the house. Miep has her exams next Tuesday, she needs me too. I have to tutor Bertie every day. Aat is down, has to be cheered up. The atmosphere at home has to be improved. Father so depressed without his darling wife. Omi misses her and cries a lot. My friend Hansie is also in hospital, I have to visit her too.

I did not see much of Jules; he left for his job very early every morning, as soon as the curfew for Jews allowed. The way we got round the curfew was to invite friends over to our house. The Jewish kids would stay the night; the others would go home, for if you weren't Jewish you did not have to be off the streets until midnight. Nevertheless, the restrictions were beginning to close in on me. When I visited Mother at the hospital, it would all spill out – the rage, the hurt, the rotten feeling of being left out.

It isn't very nice, to look over at the tennis courts and to know that you can't go in. You see your friends on their way to play tennis or hockey, or to go rowing or sailing, and you can't do any of those things any more. If you decide to go for a bike ride, you keep coming upon signs saying 'Forbidden to Jews'. But I still walk around proudly, with my star on my chest. We have to sew those stupid things on to every jacket, every dress we own. My head is aching, it's practically bursting. I think I'd better go and lie down. Everything will come out all right in the end. Chin up.

The headmaster of our school, Father's friend Dr Bartels, was fired because he had managed to get on the wrong side of a Nazi collaborator. Everyone was in a terrible mood about it at school. We were notified, via *The Jewish Weekly*, that all Jewish boys were required to have a physical, to be screened for work camps. Jules, who wore glasses, was rejected. We were terribly relieved, even though we had no clear idea what 'work camps' were. As for what was printed in what passed for newspapers these days – vicious attacks on Jews and their 'Jew-friends' – I couldn't believe that anyone could actually be taken in by such rubbish.

Clothing was becoming scarce. Textiles were rationed, as were shoes and other necessities. Much of the merchandise in the stores had been shipped to Germany. Meanwhile, I was growing out of my clothes at my usual rapid rate. So when I discovered a white Navy jacket in a closet, I couldn't get over my luck. The jacket had belonged to Frans Oppenheimer, the son of a friend of Mother's from Germany, who had joined the Argentine Navy when the Nazis came to power. Frans had visited us when his ship was docked in Rotterdam just before the invasion. He had left his dress suit with Mother, who was to send it to the cleaners. After Rotterdam was bombed, we knew that Frans would not be coming back for his suit until the war was over.

The jacket was a perfect fit for me. My parents told me I could wear it. 'Frans will definitely understand,' they said. 'We'll buy him a new one after the war.'

I felt very stylish in my white coat with its shiny brass buttons. No one noticed that it buttoned the wrong way. I sewed the yellow star on the breast pocket. I looked like a one-star general.

One day, walking home arm in arm with my friend Noeke, I heard a bicycle coming up behind us on the pavement. Suddenly I felt a punch in my back, and a blow to my head. At first I thought it was a friend wanting to surprise me, but I realized this was no friendly pat. The person on the bicycle did not stop, but pedalled on furiously. I ran after him, yelling, '. . . *Bastard!*' I tried to grab the luggage rack on the back of his bike, but then I heard Noeke yelling, 'Edith! Come back! You can't win! Let the creep go!' I stopped, disappointed and angry. I couldn't figure out why anyone would want to hurt me – especially someone who didn't even know me.

Noeke took my arm and said, 'Come on. Let's go. They won't scare me off that easily. I'll always be your friend.' And then I understood. The white blazer with the brass buttons and the yellow star. And my friend Noeke, with her blonde curls and nothing sewn on *her* coat. To me, the star had always been a badge of honour. Now I knew that others did not necessarily see it that way.

11

The End is Near

2–3 June 1942. 1.30 a.m.
I feel the end is near. Not my end, but the end of the war. I can't sleep. For the past hour squadrons of aeroplanes have been flying overhead. English planes. On their way to Germany. They have been coming for the past three nights. Cologne and Essen have been bombed. I wonder which city is going to get it tonight? It's a loud, constant drone. Some bombs have been dropped over The Hague as well. Even so, it's a comfort, to me.

I would lie awake at night waiting for my 'friends' to return and bomb the dickens out of the Germans over the border. The bombing raids were a sign, at least, that somebody out there was doing something!

6 June 1942
I just had a good cry on Father's shoulder. If only Mother could come home! I miss her so terribly. If only the war would be over.
    Dear God, please come and help us!

Even parties and fun were not the same any more.

15 June 1942
Today it was Dick's birthday. He is eighteen. The whole

crowd was there. Real chocolate ice-cream with whipped cream on top! It was a wonderful evening.

Yet I am not in the mood these days. I am not that happy. I feel all bunched up inside, just as if something very heavy is pressing on my chest. Everyone is down. Jewish boys are being screened for work camps. That's a kind of hell, if you are sent there. Thank God Jules has been turned down. Gerard received notice that he's been selected. But he isn't falling to pieces about it. I am really fond of that boy.

Miep had a great time at the party. Well, sure, she can still have everything she wants. If she wants to go and play tennis or hockey, she can. If she wants to go away on holiday, or on a school outing, then she can do that. Meanwhile, we're prisoners here. No more sailing, rowing, biking, soon not a single thing. But I'll stay strong! Only sometimes I wonder, 'Where is the sunny disposition you used to have, Edith?' Other people come to me with their problems and their troubles. I love to help them. But still . . . how I long for a time when we'll all be carefree again!

Mother's surgery had gone well according to her doctors, but she was now encased in plaster from her armpits to her toes. A young resident had decorated her cast by planting a little red, white and blue flag on her toe. A metal pin had been inserted into the bone below her knee as an anchoring point for the traction machinery that was to keep her hip immobilized for several months. Mother took it all in her stride, and never complained. My trips to the hospital were always the high point of my day.

Wonderful hours, those, that I spend by her side. Mother is so incredibly giving; she gives me so much strength and support.

Some things, however, were so bad that I could not even put them in my diary. By refusing to record them, I managed to convince myself they never happened. My recollections of this period were skewed towards examples of loyalty and courage shown by friends and strangers. If something did not fit in with this glowing picture of my fellow countrymen, I refused to process it.

This 'selective amnesia' became clear seventeen years later, at a high school reunion in The Hague. A former Netherlands Lyceum schoolmate, whom I did not remember, came up to me and started talking about an incident that he said had haunted him for years. I asked him what he meant. 'Surely you can't have forgotten it!' he exclaimed.

Only by telling me the entire story did he manage to jog my memory. My form teacher, Mr Dommisse, had invited Hannie and myself to be present when the results of my former classmates' finals were announced. I was happy and excited to be back in the courtyard of the Netherlands Lyceum, surrounded by old friends. Suddenly I saw two figures in black shirts and trousers, shiny military boots and the despised NSB pin on their collars, marching towards us. I knew them very well: Jan S. and Rudy I., classmates of mine. They had always been less than average students, and not very popular. In the past they had always been pleased when my friends and I had included them in our activities. The transformation was startling.

'*Sieg Heil!*' they yelled at us in German, their livid faces just inches from Hannie's and mine. '*Was machen Sie hier?*'*
I was flabbergasted, and opened my mouth to reply, but no sound came out. 'You know, don't you, that you are not wanted here?' they went on, shouting hoarsely in German. 'Get out of here!'

---

* 'What are you doing here?'

Two boys from my class started pushing Jan and Rudy out of the way, but the teachers quickly stepped in and held them back. Mr Dommisse took Hannie and me by the arm and guided us quickly out of the courtyard, whispering, 'Come, girls, we can't win this way. Let's just go quietly.'

I walked straight to the hospital, where I knew Mother would help me get over my hurt. After my visit, she wrote me a letter in which she tried to console me.

My Dearest Eetje,

You left me yesterday in a sad mood, darling. Later I had some time to think about it all . . . Yes, my angel, when everything is going your way, there is no impetus, really, to make you change and grow. Just as God created nature and the sun to shine over the world, so that everything may look radiant and joyful, so did He also invent rain, which, depressing as it can be, is nevertheless crucial to life, since it provides us with food and water.

So it is in our own lives, darling. There are all sorts of disappointments we have to deal with, humiliations, sorrow, shame, grief, etc . . . But we also have our share of happiness, success, love and lots more. Now in your case, you just had a terrible disappointment because of the gross insult you experienced. But you must also take into account *who* did this to you, and then, my darling, perhaps you can tolerate it more easily, or rather, shrug your shoulders, and think, 'Someone like this can't insult me.' Your true friends remain your friends, and you have made plenty of those in your short life thanks to your own good qualities!

A heavy burden has been imposed on us now, on you and on thousands of others, and we must try, whatever comes, to keep our heads high . . . That will depend on our will-power and self-confidence. Yes, if we didn't have those, life would not be worth living. I compare this time that we Jews are living through now, to a little child that is being bullied by a big boy who wants to grab him and wrestle him to the ground.

Nothing lasts for ever, my dear. As long as you know that I for one am with you, and together we will head forward, with open eyes and an open heart . . . ! God will protect us if we stay true to our course, keeping in mind our responsibilities and duties to ourselves and to our fellow man.

Being home was no fun any more. I felt I should help Omi and Jacques, but I couldn't – I had to study. My orals were coming up the second week of July. Father said I could accept the Fernandes' invitation to go and stay with them for a week or two, if that would help me study. I went, grateful that he understood. It was so much easier to concentrate there. Miep's mother, Aunt Jetty, pampered me and fussed over me, and it was a great feeling to know that for a few days I was responsible only for myself.

26 June 1942
On Wednesday we all had to turn in our bicycles. Mob scene. Long queues. Lots of friends and acquaintances, of course. It was like a social event. I had to wait from half past eleven until two. Jews are not allowed to cycle any more. What a mean dirty trick. Even that they take away from you! True, but these days I keep thinking, 'Where the need is greatest, help *must* be nigh.' Last night Bremen was bombed again. When will the end finally come?

Jacques, our 'butler', was turned down for the labour camps after being screened. He seemed perfectly healthy to me. My friend Gerard was not so lucky. We heard he was being sent to a camp. The news kept going from bad to worse for us.

1–2 July 1942

New measures again. Not only are we not allowed to cycle any more, we are not allowed to ride the trams either. We have to be off the street by eight, and we are not allowed inside non-Jewish homes. Shopping is restricted for us to the hours between three and five p.m. It's a mess. It's awful for Mother, because the hospital is so far for Father and Omi to walk to. Jules was with her this afternoon. I went too, an unplanned visit: she was overjoyed. I've moved back home; I couldn't stay at the Fernandes' any more. I did have a wonderful time there. At my last meal with them last night, I read them a poem of thanks I had written. We were all so moved and depressed because of the new measures, and crying so hard about everything, that we ended up sobbing with laughter. It was a comical tragedy, really.

My old crowd at the Lyceum organized a farewell for Hannie and me, a pyjama party in a shed at the back of Loulou's property. Loulou's parents were the Baron and Baroness van Wassenaar, and they lived in a big house with lawns sloping down to a shady wood. We felt safe in the little shed, far from prying eyes. We had decided that since the shed was not a real house, Hannie and I weren't technically breaking the law against visiting Gentiles. The other girls fought over who would sleep in the bunk next to mine. Nothing had changed in our friendship – that was the message they were trying to get across. The party ended with a pony-ride through the woods the next day. Weren't we lucky, we giggled, that the Nazis had not yet thought of including pony-carts in the list of vehicles they had declared off-limits to Jews!

Finally came the day of our orals. Hannie and I had arranged to meet very early. We had to leave ourselves extra time to get to school, since we had more than an hour's walk ahead of us.

13 July 1942

I crammed until the last possible moment. Hannie and I set off for school together. It was raining. Seeing us walking along in the rain, with our stars on, an out-of-service bus stopped for us. The bus driver said he'd take us wherever we were going. It was really nice of him, but we thought it safer not to accept. We said we couldn't, because then we might land in jail, and he said, 'Well, then we'll all go to jail together, that will be a blast.' 'O K,' we said, 'but not right now, thanks: we are on our way to our finals . . .' We decided we had better get going. 'Next time perhaps, after the war,' we told him and continued on our way.

I passed with flying colours (except for chemistry, and even there I managed to just scrape through).

So there it is: I passed! There were speeches, we said goodbye to the teachers. Then straight to Mother to tell her the great news. Mother and Jules both overjoyed. Great celebration. Everyone in the hospital had heard the news. As we were leaving, Adrie appeared with flowers.

At home I received a victory welcome from Omi, Miep, Dolf. Flowers. Cakes.

Little did I know it then, but it was not just school that was finished for me. This day marked the end of my childhood. It was also the last entry in my diary. Within a week, Edith van Hessen would be no more.

12

Diving Under

For two years we had been lulled into thinking that the worst would never happen. It was an assumption that the Nazis had cleverly been using to deceive an entire population. As Father was to write to me a year later:

> It's strange how much you can bear, if your doom is parcelled out to you in small doses. It's just like poison: if you start taking it very gradually, increasing the quantity drop by drop, then your body will eventually get used to it.

It was not until the summer of '42 that it finally dawned on us that the cavalry was not on its way, and that if we were going to save ourselves, we had better do something about it – soon.

On Tuesday 14 July 1942, there was a special edition of *The Jewish Weekly* with the following declaration:

> The Sicherheitspolizei has informed us of the following:
> Some 700 Jews have been arrested today in Amsterdam. Unless the 4,000 Jews who have been assigned to labour camps in Germany report this week for transportation, these 700 hostages will be sent to a concentration camp in Germany.
> . . . Signed, A. Asscher and Professor Dr D. Cohen, Chairmen of the Jewish Council of Amsterdam*

It was this declaration that galvanized Jules into action. He had come to the conclusion that the only thing to do now was to 'dive under' – i.e. to assume a new identity – before the dreaded summons arrived for him. He convinced Father and Mother that they should let me go too. In The Hague the Germans seemed to be targeting only young men for the moment, but Jules was sure they would soon start calling up young women as well, as they were already doing in Amsterdam. The German goal appeared to be the rounding-up of all healthy young Jews, whatever their gender, for exploitation in their labour camps.†

Poor Father! As if he didn't have enough on his mind! Not only were his children in danger, his wife in hospital, his home and livelihood threatened, daily life made impossible by constant restrictions – but his own health had been deteriorating as well. He had been trying to disregard recurring problems with his throat and larynx, but he could no longer ignore the raging toothache that had been plaguing him lately. Now

---

* The leaders of the Jewish Council were faced with a difficult decision: whether to sacrifice 700 Jewish hostages for 4,000 still at large, or the reverse. The decision they came to was to encourage the 4,000 'conscripts' to report obediently for the 'labour camps' so that the 700 hostages condemned to 'concentration camps' would be set free, thus playing neatly into the Nazis' hands.

† Many people were reaching this conclusion at the same time. In Amsterdam, Anne Frank's family went into hiding on 9 July, when her sister Margot received a call-up notice; the van Daan family, with whom the Franks shared their hiding place for three years, went into hiding on 14 July.

One month later, on 7 August, another declaration made it absolutely clear what Jews were to expect. It said that any Jew who did not respond to his/her summons would be arrested and sent to the concentration camp of Mauthausen. The same punishment was in store for any Jew who was caught not wearing a star or changing residence without notifying the authorities.

that my exams were behind me, I suddenly started paying attention to what I should have noticed months ago. Seeing Father sitting there agonizing over his children's fate, more bowed and careworn than I remembered ever seeing him, clutching and rubbing his right jaw and chin, I realized that he was in immense pain. I dragged him to the dentist, who treated an ugly abscess in his mouth. Back home, I put him to bed and tried to make him as comfortable as possible.

It did not take long for Father and Mother to agree to Jules's plan. Reports of round-ups and deportations came daily. Friends were disappearing all around us. It was not always clear who had vanished of his own volition and who had been picked up by the Gestapo. There was no time to waste. We finally realized that the Nazis were capable of anything.

A day and a half of frenetic activity followed. Jules and his friends managed to obtain a cache of stolen identity cards from an underground organization – all without the 'J' stamp. Carefully the forgers substituted our passport photographs for the originals. Then, handling small rubber stamps, scissors, knives and tweezers, they painstakingly reconstructed the missing part of the official stamp which partially covered the photographs. They also managed to replace the fingerprints, which every ID card carried, on special onion-skin paper also stolen from the authorities. Once again, I was amazed by my brother's many hidden talents. Where and when had he learned to do this sort of work?

For two days, Jules's room was Counterfeit Headquarters. He and his friends forged a number of ID cards. The excuse they used for all the comings and goings at our house was the skate-sharpening machine that Jules kept in his room. This was a unique contraption which had always made Jules's room a popular destination, and so the neighbours thought nothing of it when they saw a stream of young men entering our house with their skates around their neck, even though it was the middle of July. While one of them would start grinding blades noisily, the others could get down to the serious business of forgery.

Jules planned to cycle to the east of the country and find a job as a farmhand. His ultimate goal was to make it across to England. I had some misgivings – I was afraid my brother's dark Semitic looks would give him away. But Jules was cheerfully optimistic. He wasn't worried, he said. It was the kind of adventure he relished – living by his wits and charm, camping out while working on an escape plan. It was summer, he would have a good time. But he wouldn't leave until a place was found for me.

We had started to make discreet enquiries. At first Adrie had suggested to his parents that they take me in. The Verhulsts were very fond of me, and had indicated their hope that Adrie and I would get married one day. But I could not stay at their house under a false name. It would be much too dangerous, they said. Too many of their friends and acquaintances knew me by sight; they had seen me at Adrie's brother's wedding, as well as on many other occasions.

By coincidence, the Verhulsts had friends staying with them that week, the zur Kleinsmiedes. The two families had become acquainted in the East Indies. Mr Verhulst and Mr zur Kleinsmiede had been teaching colleagues at a secondary school in Tondano on the island of Celebes (now Sulawesi).

Tine and Egbert zur Kleinsmiede had been following the predicament of the Jews with mounting dismay. They lived in Breda, a provincial town in the south of the country, with their only child, Ineke, who was four years older than me. When they mentioned to Adrie's parents that they had been thinking about taking in a Jewish girl who could then be a companion to their daughter, it seemed a stroke of luck. The Verhulsts told them, 'We know just the right girl,' and they immediately arranged for me to meet them.

Tine zur Kleinsmiede, or Mrs z.K., as I called her, was in her mid-forties. She was a formidable, proud, attractive woman with prematurely white hair and a determined set of the jaw. Her husband was fourteen years older, big, bulky and jovial, a retired high-school headmaster. They seemed nice, serious and thoughtful people. I immediately felt at ease with them.

It was decided that very evening. The z.K.s would take me in. Financial arrangements for my keep were hammered out between Father and the zur Kleinsmiedes. I didn't feel I had any choice in the matter. Once the decision was made that I should disappear, it was like boarding a roller-coaster; there was no getting off. I hoped I wouldn't have to stay in Breda for very long. I was worried about missing my family and Adrie. I packed a suitcase with some summer clothes – I was sure that I'd be home before the summer was out. I wanted to take my diary too, but Father cautioned me to leave it behind. 'You must not keep a diary while you're in hiding,' he said. 'It could give you away. It would reveal who you really are, and that would endanger not only you, but these kind people who are offering to shelter you as well.'

I could see that he had a point, and so I left my diary behind. I packed it carefully into the little black suitcase containing all my other precious diaries, and asked Miep Fernandes to keep them for me. I made her swear that she'd let no one read them while I was away.

That night, Father, Jules and I sat up late, going over the details of our flight. The Nazis had threatened that if you were called up and did not report for service, they'd make your family pay dearly for it. The Gestapo would come and arrest your parents and cart them off to concentration camps.

We did not know how bad these concentration or labour camps were: the authorities would have us believe that life there was bearable if you were healthy, able and willing to work. But there were also rumours of inhumane conditions and unspeakable horrors. We did not know what to believe, nor did we want to risk finding out for ourselves.

We decided to finesse our flight by making it look as though we had told no one of our plans. The scenario went as follows: the van Hessen children had plotted to run away together to Switzerland, without their parents' knowledge or consent. If the dreaded 'Green' police came to arrest us, Father and Mother would disclaim any knowledge of our whereabouts, or of our intention to escape.

The next day, 18 July 1942, Jules and I walked the familiar route to the hospital for the last time. Mother had been informed of the plan. She was in a semi-private room and, being a warm and sociable person, the curtain separating her bed from her neighbour's was almost always left open.

Today was different. Mother had requested the curtain be drawn, and two chairs had been placed at either side of her bed. Luckily her room-mate was occupied with her own visitors. Still, Mother cautioned that we should not discuss our plans out loud. And so began our unforgettable pantomime.

Jules sat on the right side of Mother's bed; I sat on her left. We all held hands tightly. Jules and I chattered cheerfully about our activities, as if it was a day just like any other. Mother held our hands in hers, and her grip conveyed what her voice could not utter. As we told her the latest gossip and she answered in her cheerful and matter-of-fact voice, long, meaningful looks were exchanged. Mother stroked our hair, as if she were blessing us, and, when the volume of noise next door allowed, whispered words of advice and caution. We whispered back that she should try to get better soon, but that we were glad that she was here, in this friendly hospital with the kind nuns, where she would surely be safer than anywhere else we could think of.

Finally it was time to go. Leaving that room was the most difficult thing of all. We started for the door several times, only to turn back for one more kiss, one more loving squeeze, all the while pretending we had forgotten something that we had to tell her in order to keep up the charade. 'Remember to bring me those handkerchiefs you promised me when you come back tomorrow, Edith,' she said, or, 'Jules, I forgot! I'm all out of reading material. Will you please bring me that book you were telling me about?' Her voice sounded normal and cheerful, while the tears were rolling down her cheeks. Every time I managed to take three steps towards the door, I would be drawn back, unable to cross the threshold. 'Go now!' she said. 'Go on! I'll see you tomorrow, my lovely children!' Finally we could linger no more. As we walked down the long hospital corridor, Mother's soft farewell still ringing in our ears, we kept up the charade, laughing and joking, loudly reminding each other not to forget the little errands she had requested.

That is the last image I have of my mother: prostrate in bed, imprisoned in plaster – but radiating extraordinary strength and motherly courage, her dark hair immaculately brushed and coiled, her eyes brimming with tears.

It was our last night at home. Father had decided to take sleeping pills and had given some to Omi as well. It was part of another rather naive ruse we had thought up: if the Gestapo came and demanded to know what had happened to us, Father and Omi could truthfully claim that we had left home without their knowledge, having been asleep when we sneaked out.

It was not easy to say goodbye to Father. Soberly, he told us that for once in his life he felt stumped for words. How could he give his children any advice when we were embarking on a road he himself had never taken? He tried to smile at us reassuringly, but I could see that it cost him great effort to do so. His right hand cupped his right cheek unconsciously – a gesture that filled me with concern and pity, for I knew how much that side of his face was hurting him.

I kissed his right hand and his right cheek, and then I kissed his other cheek and assured him that I would be fine. I promised I'd be back soon. So did Jules. Then we watched him as he swallowed the sleeping pills that would guarantee that he'd be fast asleep when we stole out of the house at the break of day.

Upstairs in my room I took out my nail scissors and a razor-blade. Carefully I started removing the yellow stars from all the articles of clothing we were taking with us. It was a tedious job, because the stars had been sewn on firmly – to pin them or tack them on with loose stitches was a punishable offence. I had to take great care not to leave any telltale lint or needle marks in the spot just above our hearts.

As I removed the last star, I felt a great weight lifting off me. Jules and I tiptoed down to the kitchen, and threw the miserable yellow rags into the stone sink. Then, with an entranced grin, my brother dropped a burning match on them and in no time at all the stars with their ugly black letters spelling out '*Jood*' curled into wispy black ashes. Gleefully we turned on the tap and washed what remained of our stars down the drain.

I went to sleep bubbling with excitement about the big adventure ahead, trying to avoid thinking about the wrenching fact that going on an adventure also meant leaving my parents behind.

Jules woke me at five a.m., dressed and ready to go. It was a beautiful summer morning. Omi was up. She had not taken her sleeping pill, because she could not bear not to make us breakfast on our last morning at home.

Jules left first. Someone had lent him a bike, which he had loaded up with his rucksack and camping gear. He was headed for the Veluwe region, in the east. The name on his new papers was 'Alfred van Meurs'. 'Call me Al. Or Fred,' he joked. He ran a hand through his dark hair, and jiggled the wire-rimmed glasses on his nose. 'OK. This is it. Good luck, Ee!'

We shook hands formally, then we threw our arms around each other and held each other tight. 'See you when the war is over, Eetje!' he whispered. 'Yes, sure, Alf, soon!' I tried to summon up a smile. 'Have fun!' Jauntily, he swung his leg over the saddle, and, with a wave, disappeared from sight behind the flowering hedge in our front garden.

The front garden was at its loveliest, with dew drops sparkling in the early sunlight. Omi clung to me in the dark hall. Her face was wet with tears. I took a deep breath and tried to summon up the sadness I was supposed to feel – but it wasn't there. I couldn't wait to be gone. Not to feel like a prisoner any more. Not to be a target. To be just like everybody else: *normal*.

'Don't cry,' I whispered to Omi. 'The war's going to be over soon, you'll see. We'll be back in no time at all, and our lives will go back to the way they were before.'

It was almost six a.m. Adrie arrived to pick me up. I clutched my bag tightly against my left side, covering the spot where the star used to be. That way, if any of our neighbours happened to glance out of the window, they would not notice that the star was missing. I jumped on to the back seat of Adrie's bike. Balancing my suitcase on the handlebars, his elbow squeezing the arm with which I held on to his waist, Adrie got us to the railway station in plenty of time. There we parked the bike and boarded the train for Breda.

There were plenty of German soldiers in the rush-hour crowd at the station – the ones in the green uniforms were members of the Wehrmacht, the ones in black the dreaded SS. My heart was pounding in my chest. Yet I felt free as a bird. I was wearing a light summer dress under my jacket. Adrie and I held hands, trying to act like an unremarkable young couple in love. In my wallet I had an ID card like everybody else's, without any ugly 'J' stamped on it. In my mind I rehearsed what it said, just in case anybody stopped me and asked for my papers:

Antoinette Schierboom, a.k.a. Nettie.
Birthdate: 22 July 1925.
Place of residence: Wassenaar.
Profession: Domestic help.

13

Herr Niemke

I had never been to Breda, a modest-sized city near the border with Belgium, which was known for its military academy. The z.K.s' house was a pleasant half-hour's walk from the station, along streets lined with leafy trees and gardens full of flowers. Adrie knew the way, having often visited the z.K.s with his family. When we finally turned into Cavaleriestraat (Cavalry Street), I saw on one side a row of pleasant brick semi-detached houses with large picture windows in the front. As is the custom in Holland, all the curtains were left open, permitting an unobstructed view of the neat living or dining rooms inside. If you were curious, you could see what the people living there were having for lunch.

Across the street there were no houses. Instead, I saw a fence, brick buildings . . . and German soldiers! 'The Cavalry barracks,' Adrie informed me. 'Of course it's all occupied by the Germans now.'

No one had warned me that my new home was to be in full view of German troops! Walking past, we saw groups of men in green uniforms and shiny boots swarming over the neat green lawns, behind high fences topped with fierce-looking iron spikes reaching up to the sky.

We arrived just in time for lunch. Mr and Mrs z.K. received me warmly and did their best to make me feel at ease. Ineke, their daughter, kissed Adrie on both cheeks, and then extended her hand to me. She was a pretty girl with very pale blonde hair, a delicate, rosy complexion and a sad expression round her mouth. Even though she was four years older than me, she had not yet graduated from the Gymnasium.* She had just learned that she'd failed her finals again (this had been her second try), so she would have to sit them again next year. She told me that next time she was going to make it; she was sure of it. I immediately offered to help her with the subjects that I was good at. I felt bad for her, and hoped she would not hold it against me that I had passed at the first attempt.

The house was quite a contrast with the home I had left behind. Our house in The Hague was bright and modern, with white walls, beige carpets, modern furniture and recessed light fixtures. Mother's taste for cheerful colours and Father's love of art were evident in the contemporary paintings on the walls and the vases of bright flowers everywhere.

At the zur Kleinsmiedes', a sombre cast hung over the rooms. A large dark mahogany cupboard, a sideboard laden with knick-knacks, and plush furniture upholstered in dark, muted colours were accented by Persian rugs, Indonesian brass, Chinese ginger jars and succulent plants lined up along the window-sills.

At midday a warm meal was served, whereas at home we had usually eaten sandwiches. It was a bean and chickpea dish that I had never tasted before. The newness of everything, combined with my nervousness, made me eat far more than I could digest. Soon I had a bad stomach-ache, which didn't help my mood. Adrie was kidding around with Ineke, and reminiscing about life in the Indies. Obviously, he felt very much at home there. I was unusually quiet and felt a mounting sense of dread.

---

* Dutch secondary school where Greek and Latin were compulsory subjects.

'Come,' said Mrs z.K. 'It's time for you to see your new room.' Just like at home, my room was in the attic, on the third floor. Its dormer window overlooked the back garden. There were birds chirping in the trees, which calmed me somewhat. It was a neat room, with a wooden bed, a table and chair pulled up to the window, a wardrobe, a low foot sink equipped with a cold-water tap, a porcelain wash-basin with a water jug, and a wooden towel-stand. An old sisal rug covered the floor. Adrie helped me unpack my few belongings. We were both sure I would be here only for a short time.

'Nettie, you are Ineke's best friend from up north, and you have come here to spend the month of July with us,' said Mrs z.K. when I had finished unpacking. 'When people ask, it's important for all of us to stick to the same story. Your mother is in hospital with a broken hip. That's all anyone needs to know.'

Adrie smiled, and gave my fingers a squeeze. 'Well, *Nettie*, you'd better behave yourself!' The name 'Nettie' sounded strange to me. It would be a while before I got used to it, and a few weeks before I would respond immediately when someone called me by my new name. But my hosts never slipped up: not having known me as Edith, they never had any trouble with my name. To them, I was Nettie Schierboom, and that was that.

Adrie did his best to cheer me up. He promised that he would come and visit as often as he could. He was to be the go-between for my parents and myself. Aat and his parents were the only people in the world who knew of my current whereabouts. Not even Father and Mother, not even Omi, not even Jules knew my exact address. That way, nobody would get that information out of them if they were ever interrogated.

We did not have another chance to be alone together. I wanted to cling to Adrie, to kiss him and never let him go.

But I controlled myself. When it was time for him to leave in order to catch the last train back to The Hague, Ineke and I walked him to the station. On the platform, he kissed both of us formally on the cheek. As the train steamed away along the platform and Adrie's waving arm disappeared from sight, I felt utterly bereaved. It was as if Adrie's departure had severed the last link with my happy former life.

At dinner that night I received the second shock about my new home. There were heavy footsteps on the stairs, and, alarmed, I looked around. 'Ah – You know the room next to yours, on the third floor, Nettie?' said Mr z.K. 'That is where Herr Niemke sleeps.'

'Herr Niemke?' I repeated stupidly.

'He is the German officer who has been billeted here,' Mrs z.K. explained, pursing her lips. 'We don't have a choice in the matter.'

My mouth fell open. A German officer, living right under the same roof, in the room next to mine! That was something I had not counted on. Herr Niemke's office was in the barracks across the street. The *Orts Kommandatur* (military command) had requisitioned rooms for its officers in most of the houses in the neighbourhood. On the face of it, the zur Kleinsmiedes acted coolly accommodating – as if it was no big deal to have an enemy staying in one's home. But I soon noticed that they did not try to hide their resentment at the 'hospitality' the Germans had forced upon them.

That first evening, I was violently ill. It might have been the beans at lunch, or perhaps it was something I ate at suppertime. Not only did I feel sick, but I also had a terrible headache. I tried not to show the z.K.s how bad I was feeling, and politely stayed up with them. As soon as I felt I could excuse myself, I went to my room, fell on to the bed and hid my head in the pillow. Ineke came upstairs to see if there was anything I needed, and she sat on my bed a while, chatting. Then Mrs z.K. entered with a glass of water and some aspirin. She drew the flowered calico curtains, tucked me in firmly and, kissing me on the forehead, said, 'We are happy to have you with us, Nettie. I hope you'll feel at home here.'

It was nothing like being kissed goodnight by my own mother, but it did make me feel a little better. I soon fell asleep, though not without telling myself I had to wake up by eight a.m. Mother and I had made a pact that we would think of each other every morning when the clock struck eight.

Shortly before my arrival, the z.K.s' maid had left to tend to a sick husband. Because of me, Mrs z.K. explained, they had decided not to hire a replacement. It would not be safe, as it could increase chances of arousing suspicion. At our first meeting in The Hague, I had told the z.K.s that I would do anything I could to help out in the household. I was eager to repay them for their kindness and courage in taking me in. Of course, at home I had never been much of a help to Mother or Omi, but then I had had my studies as an excuse. And such a busy social life on top of that. Here, I had nothing else to do.

Slowly I got used to my new existence. Ineke would not return to school until September, and I spent most of the day in her company. I was surprised at how quiet her life was, at how few distractions there were for a girl her age. Unlike me, Ineke was not used to having friends drop in. There were no parties or outings. She had few hobbies, was not very interested in sport, and was not on any teams. In fact, it soon became clear to me that because of her shyness, she did not really have any friends at all. While this made things easier from the point of view of hiding me, it also made for a pretty dull existence. Together we helped her mother keep the house immaculate: washing dishes, dusting furniture, and polishing great quantities of brass. To neighbours and visiting relatives, I was introduced as 'Ineke's friend from Wassenaar who is spending her summer holidays with us'. Since Ineke was known to be a loner, everyone seemed to be happy that she had a friend to do things with. We went for bicycle rides and long walks in the nearby woods. Mr z.K. had bought me an old banged-up bike with money provided by Father. What a treat that was, to have a bicycle and be able to go wherever I wanted, despite the 'Jews not wanted' signs!

One of my first chores was to take care of Herr Niemke's room. 'It is your job to tidy up the guest room, Nettie,' said Mrs z.K. the day after my arrival. 'As soon as he leaves the house, you'll make his bed, dust his room, clean the wash-basin and sweep the floor. Once a month you can take the rug outside and beat it. Oh and on Sunday mornings, you will bring him his cup of coffee.'

It soon became clear to me that when they made the decision to hide me, my protectors had concluded that Herr Niemke's presence was not a hindrance, but an advantage. The fact that I was the one who had to clean his room and bring him his coffee was such a brazen act that no one would suspect that I was Jewish.

Niemke's rather friendly, apologetic '*Guten Morgen*' and '*Guten Abend*', when he left for work or returned in the evening, were politely acknowledged by his unwilling hosts with curt nods. Ineke completely ignored him. I tried to act as normal as I could, although I wasn't sure what normal was, under the circumstances.

Every evening, Mr z.K. would stand at the front gate, one hand loosely in his trousers pocket, the other cupping one of his hand-rolled black-market cigarettes, passing the time chatting with neighbours and saying hello to passers-by. He was waiting for the enemy to return from work. He had made it his mission to enlighten this single naive German who did not have a clue about what was really going on in the world. Herr Niemke knew only as much as the Nazi propaganda machine wanted him to know – for instance, that the mighty German army was well on its way to conquering the whole of Russia. 'Oh, really?' Mr z.K. would exclaim, giving him a sad look from under his heavy, baggy eyelids. Well, then perhaps he had not heard of the serious losses the Germans were sustaining on the Russian front? On another day, Mr z.K. might casually inform Herr Niemke about the Nazis' taking of hostages, or their persecution of Jews and the deportation of many thousands of innocent people. In a friendly, jovial manner, he would always throw in a new bit of information during the nightly ritual of greeting Niemke at the gate. Niemke, for his part, refused to believe any of it. He was totally ignorant of the fate of the Jews. His retort was often, 'That cannot be! It isn't true!'

I made up my mind from the start to hate this man who was sleeping on the other side of my bedroom wall. He was a monster, representing the detested Third Reich. Yet I also appreciated the z.K.s' plan to make him my alibi. If the neighbours saw anything suspicious in my sudden arrival, they would be forced to conclude that with a German officer in the house, nobody in their right mind would dream of harbouring a Jewish girl.

After breakfast each day, I went to the third floor to make Herr Niemke's bed. On the bedside table, in a metal frame decorated with embossed forget-me-nots, was a picture of an attractive, smiling woman. Next to the photo Niemke's horn-rimmed reading glasses rested on top of a German news-paper. I twisted my head round to see pictures of smiling, saluting soldiers waving from tanks or lorries. With distaste I picked up Niemke's striped pyjamas and folded them neatly, placing them under his pillow. I was seething with anger at the man who had just slept in them. Handling his razor and toothbrush lying on the rim of the wash-basin, I expected a terrible malevolence to be unleashed from deep within me. I was ready to detest, geared to despise. But it was only a razor and a toothbrush. And a box of talcum powder.

The courtesy cup of coffee on Sundays was Mrs z.K.'s idea. It was not required by the high command, as the bed and the room had been. It was a mere token of Dutch hospitality, the only chink in Mrs z.K.'s hostile armour. I was to look the beast right in the eye. 'Show him you're not afraid,' she said. 'Knock on his door, put the coffee on the table, and leave. That's all there is to it.'

I did as I was told, and made a point of looking him straight in the eye, given the chance. The trouble was that Herr Niemke, lounging in his pyjamas, was even more embarrassed than I. He averted his gaze, and curtly expressed his thanks. Nevertheless, the situation fuelled my imagination. I found myself fantasizing that, despite the picture of his wife on the night-table, Herr Niemke would soon develop an irresistible crush on me. What a victory that would be for me and my entire race! What vindication! I pictured him falling on his knees before me one Sunday morning, and spilling out his secret passion. Gleefully I revelled in the scene, in which I would break his heart by revealing my dark secret. 'Well, I feel sorry for you, Herr Niemke,' I would say cruelly. 'The girl you love is Jewish.' 'No!' Herr Niemke would cry, a broken man. 'It cannot be!' 'Yes!' I would shout, triumphantly.

Even though the fantasies of unrequited passion and sweet revenge made the time pass less tediously for me, there was, naturally, no substance to any of this. Herr Niemke remained a silent presence, quiet and unobtrusive. He seemed willing to engage us in conversation, but try as he would, he never got beyond the daily greeting, the reluctant nod. Apart from the sound of his boots on the stairs, we hardly noticed him at all.

In the end, he was a man just like any other man. A little sad, a little lonely. He was not a monster. I almost felt sorry for him. What a pity I could not hate him after all.

Two months later, Herr Niemke was transferred to other lodgings. Mrs z.K. was summoned to the *Orts Kommandatur* headquarters for a reprimand. It was regrettable, she was told, that an officer had had to be removed from her home because she and her husband were known to be too '*Deutschfeindlich*' (hostile to Germans).

According to Mrs z.K., she gave those officers a piece of her mind right then and there. Mrs z.K. pointed out that in her house, her *home*, she was free to act as she pleased. She said that *decent* people would understand that she needed to be hospitable only to guests of her own choosing. That was the way things were done in *this* country. With that, Mrs z.K. wheeled round, her teeth clenched, her chin jutting forward like a weapon, and marched towards the door. The *Kommandant*, cowed by this formidable Dutchwoman, straightened his tie, clicked his heels, and, bowing his head, opened the door for her with a polite, '*Gnädige Frau, bitteschön.*'

The zur Kleinsmiedes were never ordered to take in a German officer again.

14

Helping Jews

It did not take me long to discover that even though Mr z.K. often put on a great show of being in charge, it was really Ineke's mother who had the upper hand. The two women had given him the nickname 'Boss', and often teased him. I, on the other hand, was careful to remain respectful, and always called him 'Mr z.K.' I felt sorry for him once I saw the discrepancy between his demeanour and his true status in the family. A power game was playing itself out between the two parents over the allegiance of their only child. Ineke almost always sided with her mother. It therefore seemed to fall on me to restore the equilibrium. I soon realized that was my role here: I was to be the child who would take Mr z.K.'s side. He loved to play the teacher, and very soon I became his compliant pupil. When his wife and daughter ganged up on him, I would speak up on his behalf. He could be very stern with me, and reprimanded me if I did something 'improper'. Acting the schoolmaster, he took great pleasure in correcting my grammar or vocabulary.

Mr z.K. had been a teacher all his life. He had met and married Mrs z.K. in the East Indies, where they both taught in local schools and where he was eventually promoted to headmaster. After he fell ill with malaria, the family was forced to return to Holland in 1933. They settled in Breda, where Mrs z.K.'s cousin ran a public school named the 'Nut-school'. The cousin, Jo Ufkes, a resolute, no-nonsense spinster, had offered Mr z.K. a teaching post, which he had gratefully accepted, since jobs were scarce at the time. But it was quite a comedown for him – from headmaster to fifth-form teacher.

Mrs z.K. was made a trustee of the school's kindergarten. The z.K.s missed their colonial days and often wistfully reminisced about the wonderful years they had had: the tennis parties, the outings, the receptions at the governor-general's mansion, the loyal servants living behind the house. In Catholic Breda, the Protestant minority formed the town élite, and Mrs z.K.'s wealthy relatives were part of that élite. I got the impression that Mr and Mrs z.K. hadn't quite made it into the inner circle of the clan.

Mr z.K. had retired from teaching just before I arrived, and these days his responsibilities were limited to grinding coffee in the morning for the strong brew his wife concocted out of her dwindling hoard of precious coffee beans (mixed with roasted chicory), and polishing the family's shoes, a task he performed with great zeal and the occasional touch of spit. He also ran errands for his wife on his bicycle. Mr z.K. was a huge presence, and wherever he went, his friendly voice could be heard booming in enthusiastic conversation with people he met in the street.

After lunch he would excuse himself, announcing that it was time to write an 'English letter'. He would be up in his study, and he was not to be disturbed. I assumed that this meant he was going to take a nap, but I discovered much later that what he really did up there was recline in his easy chair and tune his clandestine radio to the BBC. That is why he was so well informed. To be in possession of a wireless was strictly forbidden.* A nephew had assembled the radio for

---

* Mr z.K.'s brother-in-law, a bulb-grower in Lisse, was eventually caught listening to a wireless hidden in one of his barns and died in a German concentration camp.

him in a cigar box. Mr z.K. must have hidden it with great ingenuity, for it was my task to clean his study, and I never found it.

'Zur Kleinsmiede' is a German-sounding name.* One morning, when Mr z.K. opened the front gate, he found the little enamelled nameplate scratched and damaged, as if someone had been throwing stones at it. He came back into the house chuckling. He was not at all upset. 'Those boys,' he said, shaking his head. 'Incorrigible. They got it wrong, of course. But how were they to know the people who live here aren't *Moffen* (Germans)? Who can blame them! In their place, I'd have done the same thing!' To Mr z.K. this was an act of patriotism, not vandalism.

In August, Adrie came for another visit. He had a pocket full of ration cards for me, obtained on the black market through underground connections of Miep's family. I was overjoyed to see him, for even though we did not get much of an opportunity to be alone together, he was a refreshing distraction and brought with him a whiff of my former life. He also brought me a letter from Mother.

5 *August* 1942

My dear friend,

How happy I was yesterday when your friend's mother was here [Mrs Verhulst] with a bunch of beautiful roses and your sweet and loving letter. The tears were rolling down my cheeks. Child, I am happy that you are so well taken care of. Be good and sensible and do not give in to moodiness. Be grateful to these good people always. Be helpful, and give them one hundred per cent of your will-power, your love and your hard work.

My darling, I think of you day and night. I start waking

* The name translates as 'to the small smithy'.

up at 7.30 in order to be thoroughly awake at eight for our appointment. I feel you right near me then, and sometimes it's as if we are having a conversation. So keep thinking of me at eight. I'll send you strength and, through your courage, you'll give some back to me. How nice of that lady to act as a mother substitute, and of Ineke to be such a good friend. Your mother is all right. Don't worry about her. Only in this heat her cast feels like a rock. They are going to remove it on 1 September. Isn't that good news? Perhaps there will be peace by then, too. Dago and his mother are fine. Have a nice day with Adrie. Be happy, and don't worry. Don't forget to keep your hair neatly combed. Your meddling old friend has a lot to say, as usual, but that's forgivable under the circumstances, isn't it? Write as often as you can. Keep your chin up, keep your sunny outlook, Nettie, and always look happy! I hug and kiss you,

Your faithful Hilligi

In the letters that I received from my parents via Adrie and his parents, they never mentioned my name. They would call me their 'little friend', 'the friend of our son', 'Moesch', or something like that. Never Ee or Eetje, my true nicknames. They signed their letters with their initials – H. or D., or their pet names, 'Doddel' or 'Dago' for Father, and 'Hilligi' for Mother. They tried to avoid any mention of the fact that I was their child (although they did sometimes slip up). It took a while for me to get used to addressing my own parents by their surname. 'Dear Mrs van Hessen', I would write to Mother. It was even stranger to see Mr and Mrs z.K. referred to as my 'dear parents' or 'your aunt and uncle'. Ineke was my 'sister'. When I saw those words, I had to swallow hard. I hardly knew these people!

The next letter I received was dated 28 August 1942. Mother

wrote that my friends Alice Cohen and Dicky Polak had both been 'on holiday' but were now back home, because it 'hadn't worked out'. I took this to mean that they had not been successful in finding a hiding-place. She gave me news of other acquaintances and relatives who had 'gone away', which was our code for 'deported'.

> D. is very lonely, but Omi and he are coping well. Omi is full of energy, she is a wonder, I don't know where she finds the strength. My doctor just told me that tomorrow he is going to 'cut me loose'. You can understand how relieved I feel. So this is the last day of my horrible plaster trousers!

Even though Mother's cast came off, it was not the end of her confinement. She was obliged to stay in bed, and the doctors warned her not to move. She could not get up and walk around, as she had hoped. Also, she worried increasingly about Father. Yet she always managed to sound optimistic and even cheerful.

31 August 1942
My faithful dearest one,

I am so happy to hear how content you are. God has never abandoned me and I feel now that I am truly one of the Chosen Ones because he is protecting my children. You know, my treasure, that I was never very devout and only a true believer. But these days, I pray for all of you to my dear Lord, because in my loneliness I feel his presence more than ever, and those who worship him, he will never abandon.

For D. it is not the same. It's very quiet at home. He seems at a loss. He would have preferred a lot of noise and the garden filled with young people, as before. The telephone does not ring; the doorbell is quiet. Well, that too will come again.

I am glad you have found such a good friend in Ineke. Later she'll have to spend a holiday with us or I'll send both of you to England (if we still have any money by then). Once the war is over . . .

Read in your spare time. Read good books, darling. Don't worry about us. There's no reason for that yet. May God protect our men. Be good . . . and be careful.

In her next letter, she revealed that Adrie had seen Jules, a.k.a. Alfred van Meurs:

I squeezed Adrie dry like a lemon when he came last Sunday after he'd seen Alf. Adrie really is such a nice boy. Every chance he gets, he drops in to tell me something or to keep me company. He cheers me up, or he'll ride over to see Father or Omi . . . he is so loyal. His sweet mother too. I am looking forward to the letter that she'll bring me. That's the only pleasure I have right now, that and dreaming with Aat about the great party that we will give for all you young people when the war is over . . .

But I am worried about D. Always that tooth of his. Now it has grown into such an abscess that it needs to be irradiated. He'll be treated in this hospital, so I shall see him two or three times a week.

Adrie had cut short a sailing trip through Friesland in order to bring Mother news of Alfred/Jules, whom he had arranged to meet somewhere in the countryside. His companions on the sailing trip were Miep, Ineke and several other friends of ours. When Adrie had suggested that Ineke come along, I had enthusiastically encouraged her to take him up on the invitation. She had so little of that sort of fun in her life. I did not complain about being left behind. I was trying very hard to be a good sport.

*

Mr z.K. had had a Jewish colleague at his old school, a French teacher called Mr Gokkes. He had lost his post the year before, when all Jewish professors had been dismissed. He was now working at Breda's Jewish Council, a bureau set up in every town by the Germans to facilitate communications with the Jewish inhabitants. He had a young wife and a two-year-old son named David. My hosts were very concerned about the Gokkes family, and kept in almost daily touch with them.

One afternoon, when I had finished my chores, Mrs z.K. gave me permission to go over to Mrs Gokkes's house to help her a little. I had never met the family, but I had heard from the z.K.s that Mrs Gokkes was having a hard time. Jews were no longer permitted to keep non-Jewish help, and were allowed to shop for food only during a two-hour period in the late afternoon. I had suggested that I go over there to lend a hand. I was secretly eager to meet her.

I was received by a young and very weary woman. 'Hi, I'm Nettie,' I said.

'Nettie! How awfully nice of you to come and visit me!' she exclaimed. She wore a flowered apron with the familiar yellow Star of David sewn over her left breast. Her friendliness bordered on servility. I recognized the attitude. It was similar to the feelings I had experienced only a few short weeks earlier towards all the non-Jews who had gone out of their way to show me their sympathy or compassion. But now it made me extremely uncomfortable. I tried to act diffidently, as if it was the most normal thing in the world for a non-Jewish girl like me to come to her aid.

While Mrs Gokkes went shopping, I stayed home and played with little David. He too had a big yellow star covering almost the entire front of his little polka-dotted overalls. Motivated by a sense of obligation or guilt, I cleaned up the kitchen and tried to tidy up the messy living room. I wanted to surprise Mrs Gokkes. When she returned, I was peeling potatoes while telling David a story. When she saw me, she said, 'Oh, but wait, Nettie! Don't spoil your dress. Here, put this on!' Before I could say a word, she had slipped her apron over my head and tied its strings around my waist.

As I continued to peel the potatoes, she gave me a startled look and began to laugh. 'Heavens!' she said, clapping one hand over her mouth and pointing her other hand at me. 'Look at you! Now you look just like a Jew!'

I glanced down and saw the hated yellow star on my chest. I searched her face to see if she suspected anything, but her amusement was genuine and innocent, so I forced myself to laugh heartily along with her. Later, over a cup of powdered imitation tea, she was embarrassingly grateful for all the work I had done. I wanted to shout, 'Stop it! It's not necessary! It's nothing special! I am Jewish too and I know exactly how you feel!' Instead, I smiled and waved her words away, muttering, 'Don't mention it. Glad to help.'

Before going home, I offered to take the rubbish out to the street for the next day's collection. When I came back inside, I grabbed my jacket, promising to be back soon. Mrs Gokkes pointed at me, smiling. 'Don't forget to take off my apron,' she said.

At dinner that evening, chuckling, I told the z.K.s the story of the apron. Mr z.K.'s face turned white. 'You are never to go there again,' he said emphatically. I started to protest. But both Mr and Mrs z.K. were adamant. 'What if the Gestapo raids the house while you are there, star or no star? How are you going to convince them you are *not* a Jew? Do you really want to subject your forged identity card to that sort of scrutiny?'

Crushed, I felt as if another link to my past had been broken. However, the danger, I realized, was not only to myself. The z.K.s were risking imprisonment and even death in harbouring me. I had little choice but to obey.

A week later, the Gestapo came for the Gokkes family.

They barely had time to hand little David over the fence into a neighbour's outstretched arms.

After what happened to the Gokkes family, the remainder of Breda's small Jewish community felt even more threatened. Nobody knew who would be next. Mr and Mrs z.K. turned their attention to another Jewish family they were friends with, the Koperbergs – Leo, Hanny and their thirteen-year-old daughter Tineke. It was decided that it was time for the Koperbergs to go into hiding. There was no time to lose. A hiding place for the Koperbergs had been found in the Bics- bosch, a rather impenetrable marshland to the north of Breda.* Financial arrangements had been made with a farmer who agreed to let the Koperbergs have a very small room in his barn. There was a hatch in the wooden floor leading to a cramped hiding place in case of danger.

One dark and rainy evening, the Koperbergs, wearing macs, sneaked into our house. Three black-market bicycles were wait- ing for them in the z.K.s' shed. The plan was for the family to spend the night with us and leave early the following morning before dawn, Mr and Mrs z.K. going along as their guides. I was excited for them – I knew not only what it was like to be relieved of that hated yellow star, but also how it felt to leave one's home, and the fear of being caught. When they arrived safe and sound at Cavalry Street, we breathed a sigh of relief. It felt almost like a party. Real coffee was served, with brandy and butter biscuits baked by Mrs z.K. that morning. Although our guests were apprehensive about their flight into the unknown, we all acted excited and happy. Mr Koperberg couldn't stop telling jokes which had us all in stitches.

* The Biesbosch, spanning the delta of the river Maas (Meuse), was a popular hiding place for the underground and other fugitives. If you were not familiar with the treacherous tides, it could be very dangerous. A good number of Germans drowned there during the occupation.

Suddenly the doorbell rang. We all froze. It was late, after eleven. Who could that be? The heavy velvet curtains were drawn; we could not see outside.

The Koperbergs dived behind the sofa. Mrs z.K. got up and went to the front door. My heart was beating wildly. I looked around, hesitating. I wanted to hide too, but if I did, wasn't that giving myself away? The Koperbergs did not know, and were not supposed to know, that I was Jewish. Clenching my teeth, I just stayed where I was. A man's voice was heard, calm, politely insistent. He was speaking in German. I noticed Mr z.K. looking at me, and Ineke biting her nails. I was sure everyone could hear my heart pounding.

Then we heard Mrs z.K.'s voice: '*Vielen Dank. Danke-schön.*' The door closed. The key was turned in the lock. Mrs z.K. came back into the room, wiping her forehead with her handkerchief. Six pale faces were turned towards her.

'It's nothing. He's gone. A German soldier. He noticed a glimmer of light coming from the side of the house. He just stopped to warn us, so that we wouldn't get into trouble with the authorities.'[*]

A nice German! He didn't want us to get into trouble! We couldn't believe it. 'Nettie,' Mrs z.K. said, turning to me, 'it's the light in the bicycle shed. Someone must have left it on. Please go and turn it off immediately.' As I jumped up to do so, I noticed Mr z.K. shaking his head at me reproachfully. Nothing more was said about who had forgotten to turn off that light. The grown-ups had another drink and then everybody went to bed. The Koperbergs and their guides were to leave the house at the crack of dawn.

---

[*] The German authorities were very strict about the total blackout at night, demanding absolute compliance.

15

The Messengers

September came, and Ineke went back to school. The end of the war was nowhere in sight, and we realized that my stay in Breda was not just for the summer. But I never felt that my protectors resented my presence, or that they were eager for me to go home. Still, heeding my parents' advice, I tried to show my gratitude by working as hard as I possibly could.

With Ineke leaving early in the morning and needing to concentrate on her studies when she returned home, I now took over all the household chores that we had been sharing equally over the summer. The large house kept me busy from dawn until dusk. I was getting quite a domestic education from Mrs z.K. She showed me how to darn socks, how to beat the dust out of carpets, and how to polish the brass finger bowls that were always set out at dinner next to our plates, no matter how meagre the meal.

Helping to prepare the meals was the high point of my day. We did not go hungry, but food was definitely limited. Breakfast consisted of four slices of bread each, with one thin slice of cheese or some jam. We always had a cooked meal at lunchtime – soup, potatoes or beans, with whatever modest ration of meat, eggs or fish was obtainable that week – and bread again in the evening, with some thinly sliced cold cuts if available. For a special treat, we might occasionally open one of the tins of pre-war sardines that Mrs z.K. kept in her cellar.

I ate my bread very slowly, because I did not want to be the first to finish. That way I didn't have to look on while the others were still eating. Sitting round the table, the curtains open, in full view of passers-by on the street, we were very aware of our table manners. Mr and Mrs z.K. were particularly strict about the proper way to hold a fork or sit at the table. There was a ritual about how the food was served that took some getting used to on my part. Our entertainment consisted of watching the people who passed by, and commenting on their demeanour, whether they looked in and greeted us or whether they walked by, unaware of our eight eyes following them. Other than that, we just concentrated on our food. A favourite topic of conversation was the z.K.s' frequent pre-war visits to France. Mrs z.K. was a Francophile, and she and her husband had explored that country diligently and methodically. By the end of my stay in Breda, I was able to bring up favourite anecdotes about their French holidays as if I had been there myself.

The next-door neighbours had three young daughters, all studying the piano. Their *études* and *sonatines* sounded regularly through the common wall and it was not long before I could figure out exactly which of the sisters was at the keyboard. Ineke, too, was taking piano lessons, and played some of the very same pieces that we heard from next door. With all that music around, I was drawn to trying my own hand at it. I had been taking piano lessons ever since my parents had given me a baby grand two years earlier, and soon my own stumbling attempts at the same music could be heard throughout both houses. I was happy when it went well, when I could lose myself in the music; it was one of my few forms of entertainment.

Visitors were another welcome though rare distraction. When one of Mrs z.K.'s three cousins, Jo, Riek or Ine Ufkes came around, out would come the silver teapot and the best china. Mrs z.K. would pour the tea, and I would offer the guests a biscuit from a fancy tin. A second cup of tea was followed by a second biscuit or, before food became very scarce, perhaps a piece of chocolate. Everything was measured: one each – no less, no more. After the tea ceremony it was time to offer the guests a drink. When they had finished their carefully measured drink, everyone knew it was time to go. The guests would stand up, shake hands, and leave. The z.K.s would sometimes return the visit. But I never went along, and I never saw the inside of their houses. If I had been invited, Mrs z.K. would have declined for me, explaining that Nettie was 'visiting her parents'.

Occasionally Mr and Mrs z.K. left early in the morning for a 'nice ride in the country'. We knew what that meant: they were going to visit the Koperbergs. The farm where the Koperbergs were hidden was a long and difficult bicycle ride away. To get there, you had to take a rope-ferry across the water; the ferryman's pockets were lined with generous tips from Mr z.K. to ward off any suspicious enquiries. The z.K.s were the Koperbergs' only contact with the outside world. (The motivation of the farmer who hid them was purely financial; aside from giving them shelter, he washed his hands of them.) On these visits their friends would bring them news of the war, encouragement and hope – as well as the foodstuffs hidden in their bicycle baskets and coat pockets. I would have given anything to have made the trip to the Koperbergs myself, but that had been ruled out from the start. By now I knew better than to insist.

I began to savour being alone in my room. Only there could I be myself – spunky Edith, instead of obedient Nettie. I wrote letters to my parents, and to Adrie and Miep, hoarding my little pile of finished letters until the next visit by one of the couriers, Adrie or his parents – our only means of mail delivery. I wasn't allowed to have any photographs of my family in my room – only Adrie's photo was permitted. I would kiss his picture before I went to sleep, which helped me to feel less alone. I did keep the letters that my parents wrote to me, and these I read over and over again until I practically knew them by heart. (Mother insisted that I should burn them after reading them, but I could not bring myself to do it. My obedience did not go that far. I hid the letters under a pile of clothes in my cupboard.) I also doodled for my own amusement, sketches or poems, but much less often than at home. Here nobody was particularly impressed by or interested in my creative pursuits. I seldom received a compliment for my piano-playing. However, I was rewarded with a satisfied nod when my cleaning efforts were noted.

The z.K.s were an austere family, and compliments were not handed out readily. Intuitively, I had made up my mind from the start never to outshine Ineke. I helped Ineke with her maths problems. It was a subject that she hated and I loved.

I did feel free to talk about my family, and it was mainly while we washed the dishes together that I told Ineke all there was to know about my brothers, Guus and Jules, as well as about the older cousins who had often visited our house: Paul, Dolf, Renée, Hans and Otto. Soon Ineke was able to talk about members of my family as if she had known them all her life.

Ineke did not have many friends in Breda. Schoolmates were sometimes discussed at home, but I never met them. Ineke's mother tended to be critical of other people, and she was very opinionated on the subject of 'character' and 'decency'. Ineke almost always agreed with her. She could be very negative in her remarks about others. I felt that my life depended on the z.K.s and was afraid that if I didn't agree with their opinions or went against their wishes, I might risk losing their approval, and perhaps even their protection. Hence

I obediently played the role that was expected of me. The z.K.s wanted me to be a friend to Ineke – the younger sister she had never had. When she was negative about herself, I tried everything I could to cheer her up.

Her mother was always happy to see us getting along, giggling and gossiping, even if we sometimes showed a singular lack of decorum. 'That,' she'd sniff approvingly, 'shows everyone is in a good mood and everything is all right.' But sometimes Ineke's mood would change without warning, and I would find myself on the receiving end of an icy aloofness. Ineke would storm out of the room with a nasty remark, leaving me no time to respond, staring with open mouth at the door she had slammed shut behind her. At times Ineke would not speak to me for days, or address me only when absolutely necessary. I seldom learned the reason for Ineke's anger. I did wonder if it was hard for her to be forced to share her parents for the first time in her life.

Gradually I came to understand that my task was to make Ineke happy. It was a mission that was to occupy me for years to come.

When Ineke was invited to her cousin Atie's wedding, I was as excited for her as if I was going myself. Atie was marrying a young man by the name of Edzo Toxopeus, and I fantasized that it was going to be quite an elegant affair. The morning of the wedding, I made a big fuss over Ineke, making her try on a number of possible outfits, arranging her hair, trying to make her look as pretty as possible. For a wedding present, we had decorated a basket with ribbons and bows and filled it with scarce commodities – a pot of raspberry jam, a tin of sardines, 250 g of rice, a small packet of real tea and 125 g of sugar, interspersed with little nosegays. I had written an 'ode' to the young couple to go with it, and had spent some time teaching Ineke how to recite it as she handed them her gift. Pushing her out of the door as she left with her parents, I told her, 'Smile, and the world will smile with you' – the words my mother used to whisper in my ear whenever she caught me looking sullen or unhappy.

I walked back inside and started washing the breakfast dishes. I pictured Ineke, surrounded by relatives, smiling and having fun, with her family all intact. I imagined her reciting the poem I had written for her. I was alone in the house. I began singing a happy song, telling myself I was no poor Cinderella, but a Svengali. Besides, my time would come.

When the zur Kleinsmiedes returned from the wedding, no one mentioned my ode. The wedding 'had gone off rather well'. That was all that was said. Later, when I asked Ineke if the young bridal pair had liked the poem, she shrugged and said, 'I think so.'

'Idiot!' I scolded myself. I realized that I could not live Ineke's life for her, nor could I expect her to live mine.

The first time the messengers appeared was about two months after my arrival in Breda. Adrie's parents, whom I called Uncle Aa and Aunt Dop, arrived for a short visit. Without wasting any time, Aunt Dop put her hands on my shoulders and said, 'Nettie, something serious has happened.'

I froze, not wanting to hear any bad news. Gently she went on, making me look at her, 'Your father and grandmother have been thrown out of the house in de Mildestraat. The Germans came and confiscated it. They are staying at the Thalheimers' house for now.' The Thalheimers were Jewish friends of my parents who had lived round the corner from us. They had fled to Switzerland at the beginning of July.

As soon as I could excuse myself, I raced upstairs to read the letter she had brought for me. Mother had written:

Friday
My angel, my Moeschele,

Much has happened as no doubt that darling Mrs Ver-hulst has already told you. But I can breathe a sigh of relief again, because my beloved old mother and our darling angel D. don't have to go to prison and from there, undoubtedly, to Poland.

Just imagine: last Wednesday, D. was resting on the couch after his radiation treatment. Omi was out, on her way to visit me. Someone rings the doorbell. Looking out of the window, D. sees two Dutch policemen. 'Oh God, they've come to get me ... because of the children ...' Father opened the door. 'You must vacate this house within one hour, and you and your mother-in-law are to report to the House of Detention.' Father remained outwardly calm, and invited the men to come in and sit down. He started telling them his story, about the children who ran away, his wife in hospital, etc, etc. But to no avail. 'Go pack your bags. For Poland,' they said. Father went upstairs to his study to fetch his papers. Suddenly he notices, through the open window, Mrs Keyser entering the front garden. You remember her, she's the sister-in-law of the girl you were tutoring this spring. Anyway, he shouted at her, 'Go away, the police are here. Don't let them get you too!' 'I know, that's why I came,' she called back.

So nothing happened, at least for now. Who knows what else is still to come in this world! In any case, my good Moeschele, don't you worry. The good Lord was with us again this time.

My pupil Bertie's brother, Mr Keyser, had an important position on the Jewish Council. When he heard that the police were at our house, he hurriedly sent his wife over with papers exempting Father and Omi from deportation. But the house was confiscated, and all our belongings too. Father managed to rescue the one piece he most cared about – the terracotta bust of Mother. Our neighbour Mr Jansen had come to the back door to see if there was anything he could do, and Father thrust the sculpture into his hands.*

In her next letter, written on Rosh Hashana, the Jewish New Year, Mother repeated how lucky Father and Omi were to have been let go. In Amsterdam, Jews were being rounded up by the hundreds. My cousin Renée, who had married her fiancé in haste because there had been a rumour that only single young people would be called up for labour camps, had been picked up, together with her new husband. As for our beloved house, a German officer and his girlfriend had already moved in.

Saturday morning, New Year's Day
What a sorry state of affairs, all of us dispersed into different corners of the globe . . . what a change from the holidays that I remember! But . . . I am convinced that everything will turn out all right. Uncle Lex was here to congratulate me on the fact that Paps and Omi are free; because in Amsterdam and everywhere, in fact, people are being sent away in droves! Emmy Goldschalk and her husband, all of the Musaphs, and – don't be shocked, darling – Renée and her husband too. I heard this morning, from Aunt Marie. Everyone here is in danger. Old and young. When will it be over? For the time being I shall remain *here*, it will take me a few months to learn to walk again . . . Perhaps you will be able to help me yourself?

---

* Had it remained in our house, the bust probably would have survived, with Father's other artwork, in our attic. As it happened, the Jansens were evacuated to the Bezuidenhout quarter when our neighbourhood was declared a fortress. All their belongings, including Father's sculpture, were destroyed in an Allied bombing raid towards the end of the war.

D. is coming to visit me today. Those are my best hours. You were right, darling, to hide your diaries. Everything that I own stayed behind, and now it's gone. By the next day a blond 'you-know-what' had already moved into our house! But so what – I've already put it behind me. The thing about Renée is much worse. I cannot get her out of my mind.

I hope you realize how lucky you are. Your good fortune is one in a million. Believe me. It's up to you now to keep spreading *love* around you. Without knowing it, you have been our sun . . . It's because of you that this worked out so well (with Mrs Keyser), because you gave lessons to that child; you brought me Uncle Lex and now also those wonderful people the Verhulsts and your kind foster parents . . . My dear child, you are a '*bemazzelte*' [lucky one]!

Take care that you dress nicely. You were wearing a rather peculiar outfit in the snapshots you sent. Darling girl, try to be neat and attractive: your hair, your dress, stockings and shoes are so important. That is your calling card! I'll send you some stockings. Do you need anything else?

On the bottom, Father had scribbled this message:

If this is all we have to endure, then I think I'll be able to cope with it. Omi and I are fine. Don't worry about us. The same thing has been happening to many people you know these last weeks. If only your mother were well enough to leave the hospital soon so that she could be with me again, I would stop complaining for ever.

Three weeks later they came again, the messengers. This time to inform me that Father had cancer of the jaw. He had been rushed to a clinic specializing in maxillary surgery, the Stads Academisch Ziekenhuis, in the city of Utrecht. The specialist didn't mince his words. 'You are very late in coming to me with this. To catch the tumour, we'll have to take more than half of your entire jaw.'

Mother wrote:

Doddeltje has been in a lot of pain, but luckily they were able to give him anaesthesia, which at first they thought would not be possible. When it was all over, he asked, 'Has it started yet?' He sent word to me right after the surgery, which calmed me somewhat; still, my heart was heavy and still is, because I can't be with him. As you know, our love always meant being there for each other – now he misses me terribly and is depressed because I cannot be there to take care of him. Lots of friends have gone to visit him. Only . . . you and I . . . how my heart breaks sometimes. Still, he only has to stay there ten days, then he can go home (nebbish, what 'home'?).

You are still too young, darling, to know that tumours can be malignant. (Read the book about Madame Curie. You will understand everything much better then.) The day of the surgery I sent the surgeon a telegram: 'Doctor, please save my husband; I beg you. God be with you.' It got there just before the surgery. They had to make a long incision in his right cheek. Naturally, eating is very difficult for him now. He can only take fluids. When he is healed, they'll make him a prosthesis out of silver, into which new teeth can be set. That it was our darling, the best and most lovable angel in the world who had to undergo this . . . Omi is very shaken by all that's happened. Poor soul. But even at her age, there is no choice, one *has* to accept. We have much to bear: nothing was saved from our house, everything lost, yet perhaps your friend Alice envies us, because their lot is . . . who knows? . . . so much worse . . .*

---

* Alice and her family had been deported to Poland. They were never heard from again.

I took Mother's exhortations very much to heart, and did my best to be stoic in face of all the bad news. The zur Kleinsmiedes were not given to hand-wringing or weeping: nor would I be. I got down to scrubbing the kitchen floor with so much vigour that it made my shoulders ache. I did not want the others to feel sorry for me. Here, finally, I felt, was the adversity I had been 'training' myself for over the last couple of years. I had worked so hard on improving my character and making myself strong that I now took Mrs z.K. as my role model – stern, rigid and unafraid – rather than my parents, in whose letters, despite all the sentimental words of wisdom and encouragement, I was beginning to sense a note of despair.

16 October 1942
My dear little friend,
    You must have been astonished to hear that your old friend had to be operated on so suddenly. After more than four weeks I'm still here, and will probably have to stay a few more. The important thing is to be patient and have courage.
    Yes darling, the world does seem to be all upside down, but there is still one God who directs everything and you'll see that everything will turn out all right in the end. Now is the time to show what stuff one is made of; this is a time when strong character is moulded. One must not lose courage. I was facing a fatal decision about my life, and I had to ask myself why I should accept all this suffering. And see now, I have accepted it for the sake of my loved ones. The pain is bearable, and I keep thinking of my dear Hilde, who has been carrying her own burden so bravely, and who convinces me to put my trust in God.
    So my dear friend, don't ever despair. The sun will shine upon humankind again one day. And even if things seem too hard to bear, keep your courage, there will come a time

of comfort and happiness, as sure as God is in heaven. I wish I could be of more support to you. Alas I myself am helpless. Your letters and Hilde's are a greater comfort to me than I can give to you. Give my greetings to your dear mother and in the darkest hours, think of your faithful old friend who from far away still wishes to be in the closest contact with you. Goodbye my friend, I embrace you and press your hand in mine most warmly.

Your
Doddel

Mother thought it a blessing that Father was now safely confined to the hospital in Utrecht. Thousands of Jews had been rounded up in The Hague, and sent to unknown destinations. No one was safe any more. Almost all my Jewish friends had disappeared. As for Omi, Mother placed all her hopes in the cross that Omi had been awarded by Hitler for sacrificing her son for the *Vaterland* in the First World War. Surely that would protect her. 'I am living in constant fear for her,' Mother wrote.

My most beloved Moeschele,

I received your letter, my angel, and was moved. Of course I didn't think your idea was crazy – in fact, I had made the same suggestion to the doctor.* But he led me to understand that it would have to be Doddeltje's own bone.

The poor dear! And I can't do anything for him . . . that's the worst thing for me, believe me. Not to be able to sit by him or stroke him or take things in hand, his healing process, to make arrangements, talk to the doctors . . . *enfin*, it's terrible for me. But if the good Lord wants it so . . . I'd rather he remained in that hospital a while longer, because last night they were at it again, picking up people. I think

* I had proposed donating bone from my body to Father for a prosthesis.

all of The Hague must be empty by now. They took 1,800, I heard. Omi was here yesterday. How I pity the poor soul. They were up all night, waiting to see if they would be next. That's no way to live. God grant that nothing happens to her; may the Hitler Cross continue protecting her. They have been taking old people of eighty-five as well as pregnant women. So nobody is safe any more if you are Jewish.

That is why I thank God that you aren't with me now. That was the best thing you could have done. I was terribly unhappy at first, but now I thank God every day!

Mother felt guilty about burdening me with her sorrows and fears, but it was flattering that she considered me mature enough to confide in.

Moeschele darling,

I have always treated you like a friend and tried to be open with you about everything. Now it has reached the point where I don't keep any secrets from you, my love. As good and faithful friends we are here to advise and help each other. We are equals now and that is why I told you everything and confided my greatest fears to you. Afterwards I was sorry, and thought, 'How could I have made that child worry . . .' But where else should I unburden my soul than to you, my angel? You understand me and you are my best consolation. But now you must not worry any more and just keep doing your work as well as you can, because you are so lucky to have landed among people like these. Mrs [zur Kleinsmiede] made a wonderful impression on me when she was here and when she left I blessed her silently . . . she is my child's saviour . . . Where can you find people like that these days? Most of them are too scared.

Mother's other great worry was Jules, '. . . because he doesn't know fear. And that's wrong.' She fretted over both her children's lack of warm clothes for the coming winter and asked my aunt in Amsterdam to send me any winter clothes poor deported Renée might have left behind. Despite the great distance that lay between us, she could not stop herself from mothering me. Her advice and loving attention provided more warmth than any winter clothes.

It's so strange, that of all the pieces you could be playing, you chose Bach's *Frühlings Erwachen*. Do you know that was the first piece I mastered when I learned to play? It was my father's favourite piece of music. Whenever he had worries, I would play it for him and that always made him feel better. Omi cried when I told her. Don't forget to go to a wool shop and have them knit a pair of socks for you. Your mother says it doesn't matter what it costs, but you must be warm! And have the other things I am sending you altered to your size. Because when you go out you must look impeccable! Buy yourself some Vitamin C. And take some deep breaths every day.

Writing had long been an important part of my life. Now that I could no longer confide in my diary, I poured my heart out in my letters to my parents and my friends. I secretly kept the letters my parents sent me – it was my one and only act of defiance – but Father and Mother carefully destroyed every letter I sent them after reading it, as did Adrie and Miep. The knowledge that this was so, combined with the zur Kleinsmiedes' lack of interest in my brand of creative self-expression, particularly anything that might accidentally reveal something about my true identity, resulted in my becoming painfully muzzled. Sometimes I felt I was suffocating. I wanted to shout out from the rooftops all the things I was not allowed to say. Instead I withdrew into myself. I became more like Ineke: a good, quiet girl, watchful, retiring and obedient. At home, cared for and encouraged by Mother, the bad moods and stomach cramps that came with my period had been a reason for staying home from school and getting pampered, cuddled up in bed with a hot-water bottle. In Breda, I did not permit myself such an indulgence. If I had cramps, I ignored them, and soon hardly noticed them at all.

I sometimes found myself examining my face in the mirror with anxious interest. With all the Nazi propaganda about Jewish physiognomy, I had begun to wonder if my face could give me away. I had never thought of myself as 'looking Jewish'. Of all the members of my family, the only one fitting that description was Jules, whose dark looks made him stand out in a country where fair skin and blond hair were the norm. I used to wish that my nose was smaller and daintier, like a film star's, but I never associated it with my ethnic background. In my own view, I was a thoroughly Dutch girl, with reddish-blonde hair, a Dutch face and a Dutch name.

There was only one other person in Breda who knew my true identity. This was Mrs Daamen, a good friend of Mrs z.K., who lived in our street. She was my escape destination: in case of an emergency at the z.K.s, I was to knock on her door, as she would know what to do.

My foster parents' concern for total secrecy turned out to be very wise and totally justified. We started hearing stories about people who had been hiding Jews and were betrayed by well-meaning friends who could not restrain themselves from talking too much. No matter how well intentioned they were, the whispered, 'Don't tell a soul, but who would ever have thought that X was such a hero? He is hiding someone in his attic. Shh! It's a secret, mind you! Don't tell anybody. It's just between you and me . . .' invariably made its way to the wrong ears, and then it would be too late for both the fugitives and their protectors. The lives of all four of us were at risk.

After I had been at the z.K.s' a few months, people started

to wonder why I was still there. Meeting Mrs z.K. in the street, acquaintances would ask, 'How long is Nettie going to stay with you? I thought you said she was here only for the summer. Doesn't she have to get home?' They were not particularly nosy, but, living in a small community where people noticed what their neighbours were doing, it was a matter of pride to be well informed. Mrs z.K., however, was prepared for the question. She would lift her formidable chin, look squarely into the questioner's eyes, and reply with a shrug, 'Oh, but why should we send that poor child home? She hasn't got much of a home to go to. Her mother is still in hospital with that broken hip – she needs to recuperate for several more months before they will let her go home. And now her father is in Utrecht in another hospital, with cancer. Dreadful, isn't it? And they have been evicted from their home, because it was in the coastal area the Germans have decided to turn into a fortress. What is that poor girl to do all by herself? At least here she can be with her friend Ineke, and we can make sure she doesn't get into any trouble. I told her mother that we'd take good care of her for however long is necessary.'

It was an explanation that everybody seemed to accept. And to make the story more believable, I would occasionally stay an entire day in my room – for instance, when one of the neighbours came visiting. The visitor would be told that Nettie had gone to The Hague to visit her mother. Nobody seemed to suspect that we had anything to hide.

16

A Visit to Father

My flight to Breda had not brought with it the freedom I had expected. If anything, I was more of a prisoner here than in The Hague. Unlike at home, where I had always been free to shoot my mouth off, here I was guarded about what I said, even when there were no strangers around. I was free to go out; indeed, the z.K.s insisted that I do my share of grocery shopping, to show my face around town and 'just act normal'. But inside, I often faced a terrible loneliness, having no connection with anyone outside my foster home. I was afraid, too: I had heard that there were people who had taken up Jew-hunting as a sport.*

The war had made shopping for food a major chore. To be sure not to miss any of the scarce supplies when they came into the shops, housewives had to shop often, and pay attention to tips and gossip heard while waiting in queues. Mrs z.K. decided that my daily task should be to visit the grocer in Marathonstraat, and the corner bakery. One day on my way to the grocer's, I noticed a man standing in a window, watching me. When I came out of the shop, he was still there. Still watching me. Why?

I hurried home, scolding myself for being such a coward. But the next day, he was there again. This time when I got

---

* In Amsterdam special search-teams were formed to hunt out hidden persons. Some were paid the princely sum of Fl. 7.50 per head.

home I told Mrs z.K. about the man at the window. 'I am not going to go out any more!' I said through clenched teeth.

'Nonsense!' she said. 'If there is any danger, if that man is really spying on you, don't you think that by not coming back, you'll arouse his suspicions even more?'

The following morning, I refused to come downstairs. 'There are too many Nazi Jew-hunters out there,' I said. 'I'm safer staying in my room from now on.'

I shall never forget Mrs z.K. standing at the bottom of the stairs, aiming her pointed index finger at the floor like a gun. 'You come downstairs right this minute, young woman. Put on your coat. You are going out. The grocer knows you: you are one of his regular customers. If you don't go, we'll miss any supplies he might be keeping for his "regulars". I *forbid* you to be afraid, do you hear? Square your shoulders, keep your head high and show them how fearless you are!'

Sheepishly I stumbled downstairs, and put on my coat. I was more afraid of Mrs z.K. than of any Nazi. Relenting, Mrs z.K. decided to go with me – 'just this once!' – to be on the safe side.

The man at the window was gone.

Mother's frequent letters kept me up to date on what was happening in The Hague, which was being turned into a fortress to protect the occupiers from possible Allied sea attacks. Most of the houses in our neighbourhood had been evacuated, and many were being pulled down. Mother was torn between gratitude to Adrie, who was one of her most loyal visitors and our main go-between, and her motherly anxiety for me. I had begun to complain that Adrie and I were running out of things to say to each other, and while reassuring me that it couldn't have anything to do with me (I was always a chatterbox), she worried that I was too young to get deeply involved with a boy, the first one I had ever really loved. But these were unusual times, and Adrie and his family were in a sense our lifeline.

(Early December 1942)
My dear, beloved child, my Moeschele,

I was so happy, happier than I have been in a long time, when I received your lovely letter [via Adrie]. I don't want to be a complainer, I want to be stoic. Yet I have to tell you that I often find it very hard. And the day I received your letter was such a day. But your letter and my friend (yes, he is now my friend too!) cheered me up no end. I have come to know him so well that I understand your feelings for him. But darling, there is a war going on and I'd rather you didn't concentrate so intensely on your feelings for him. Notwithstanding that he is definitely a most lovable boy, I would not like to see you unhappy later. You are both still so young – take care that your heart does not get broken if things don't work out. Wait until these sad times are past before becoming too serious about this relationship. I want you to understand . . . I know this is not just a flirtation, my child. But I also want you to be happy and enjoy your youth. I also waited for your father during the war of 1914–18, just like the heroine in *Enoch Arden*. I didn't want anyone else and waited patiently for him until the war was over. And you have seen how happy we were.

Oh where are all the dear people we knew? There are so many I think of so often . . . And where is our Guus, my darling boy? Sometimes my heart just shrivels. I don't even know if he is a soldier . . . May God protect him!

For St Nicolaas I want you to buy something nice for Ineke. A scarf, a ring, a necklace or a book. Perhaps something for the house for her mother? I will try to rustle up some cigars for her father. Try to make it nice and festive.

I will write to them too. How grateful I am to our dear Lord that he guided you to such a good place.

12 December 1942
My dear good Moesch,

I am still moved, eight days later [after St Nicolaas] – how you have spoiled me! I look at the bed-jacket with amazement, just like I gazed at a baby of mine when it first came into the world. My Moeschele made this marvellous thing out of old wool from discarded sweaters . . . ? I had to wipe away a tear and, I'm not exaggerating, I kissed every part, both sleeves, front and back. Everyone here has had to admire your masterpiece. (Between you and me, I never would have thought you capable of it!) Did you really make this yourself, darling? It shows you this time is good for something – we are all becoming self-sufficient, re-sourceful and capable, and we understand what the word 'happiness' really means. And the poem too . . . darling, I haven't lived for nothing, if my little friend is able to come up with something so perfect.

But the best part of that evening was when Sister pushed my wheelchair to the telephone in the hall and I could talk to my Doddel for the first time in three months! There was more sobbing than talking, as you can imagine. We just exchanged tender words and endearments; there was so much to say that could not be uttered, you know what I mean. This is what has become of our traditional St Nicolaas celebration! But I slept very well last night because I felt so very *close* to all my loved ones.

D. had another operation. His mouth will remain dis-torted unless he lets them reconstruct it with a piece of his *own* bone. Maybe I'll be able to convince him to have it done after all. We must be brave.

There was more excitement this week. Omi was ordered

out of her place. (I'll have to write a novel about all this one day.) Two policemen took her away. Mrs K. called the Jewish Council to ask where they had taken her and came to see me in the afternoon. Finally, because of her 'document'* Omi was set free. She is now in a nursing home, sharing a small room with several old ladies who are in their nineties. She doesn't like it a bit and you can imagine, darling, how depressed she was when she came to visit me. But her permit to move to Amsterdam should come through any day now, and she'll be safe in the Joods Invalide.† Again it was your Mr Keyser and his wife who were her protectors. These two young people have been doing a wonderful job.

How grateful I am, my angel, that you have such a good home . . . If I had to worry about you the way I lie awake nights worrying about Alf, or when I think of my husband, who is so deserted, about Guus who is alone somewhere in the world far from us, and about Omi who is having such a hard time . . . And sometimes I do worry about Eetje too, because she needs me. But then I remember your friend Alice, her father, mother, brother, and the thousands of others who have been deported, and then one is oh, so thankful and one resists all those longings and wishes . . . while waiting for the day when these troubles will just be a memory. That day will come, that's what you have to keep reminding yourself of, my love. Of course it's difficult for you. You are going through adolescence, when a girl needs her mother most, but (and there is always a but) I prepared you for life much earlier, possibly, than other girls. I talked *everything* over with you, and that's a great advantage, which you may not realize as yet.

* The 'Cross of Honour' showing she had sacrificed a son for Germany in the First World War.
† A large Jewish nursing home in Amsterdam. One of Father's brothers was on the board of trustees and was able to pull strings to get Omi in.

Yes, my little one, keep your girlish illusions, your hopes and your dreams. You did not understand what I meant in my last letter. I don't want to take anything away from you, I only want to save you from disappointment, because the war is raging everywhere and one cannot make plans for the future. But everyone needs dreams, otherwise life would be too dull! Even I still have my dreams. To be a support, together with your dear Pa, to our children, and our children's children. I fantasize about coming to dinner at your home, your great-grandparents' silver candlesticks on the table . . . (remember that they are in safekeeping at Miep's house) . . . oh, my mouth is watering already!

1 January 1943
I didn't write to you last time a courier was here. I was suffering from homesickness . . . My longing made me restless and sentimental. I re-read 'the' speech by Doddeltje from last year (I had it with me in my writing case) and all those thoughts – 'my joy is in bits and pieces' – fluttered like nervous little birds in the darkness. But I'm over it now, darling. Whenever I think of you, my heart glows. The New Year has arrived, and I regard it as a newborn child that has yet to reveal its qualities and which we must mould in order to make something beautiful of it. The old year was terrible, of course. And still, last New Year's Eve we wished for the best. 'How is all this possible?' I sometimes ask myself. Still, it is a test from God. It was ordained; it was our turn . . . If you think of it that way, then it makes sense and we must learn to appreciate what we have. You are right, darling, it's not about parties and elegant evenings out . . . Now we know, all six of us, where our happiness lies: one for all and all for one . . . We have suffered enough, and I am praying for a speedy reunion.

I hope you had a pleasant New Year's Eve, and I *know*

where your thoughts were. I heard you can cook all sorts of things now, and I think ... My little one? A young woman is about to take the place of the little girl, like the rosebud that I was given this week which has unfurled into a beautiful flower today. As I write this, Adrie is in the next room, giving a maths lesson to a young girl. I arranged it. When he went in there, I teased him, 'Be careful! Don't fall in love!' He smiled at me. 'I can fall in love only once.' He is a dear and I am very fond of him. He told me there is a possibility you might visit D. in Utrecht. What a surprise! I am very happy for the two of you. Only I wish I could be there too. Adrie has to go. Darling, I hug and kiss you. H.

A few days before Christmas, Mrs z.K. had visited Father. It was the only time they had met apart from the day in July when they had arranged my flight. On her return, Mrs z.K. suggested that I should visit him in Utrecht. She was full of respect and admiration for Father. 'Go and see him, Nettie,' she said. 'It will do him good.'

A chance to visit Father! A chance to leave Breda and go out into the world, even if for a short time! I was wild with excitement, and also fear. Ineke was to go with me as a safeguard. Two friends on an outing. While she visited friends in Utrecht, I would stay with Flip and Joke Zwarts, good friends of my parents who had offered their home as an escape-hatch for both myself and Jules in case of trouble.

The decision to let us go had not been easy. As Mr z.K. had reminded his wife in a heated discussion, I was not safe, even with my forged papers, since those papers showed me as a resident of Wassenaar, and you were supposed to register with the police if you changed your residence or were away from home for more than a day. I was reminded again that not just my own life was at stake, but also that of Ineke and her parents.

Mrs z.K. had had some stern words of advice for us. 'You are *not* afraid, do you hear? Look every German you meet straight in the eye. Show no fear. That is the only way not to attract suspicion.'

So there I was, on a train headed for Utrecht, pretending not to be afraid. Strangely enough, I soon started to believe it myself. As I looked out at the countryside speeding by, I felt free.

I came back down to earth with a jolt. Some SS soldiers were walking down the corridor, peering suspiciously into our compartment. I had to remind myself not to be afraid. I smiled at Ineke, who smiled back bravely. I felt my knees shaking. The SS soldiers did not stop. They were only looking for a seat – thank God!

In Utrecht I was welcomed warmly by the Zwarts family. The last time I had visited them had been on a family outing in the old Chevrolet. Now Father's car was gone, as was the Zwarts family's stately townhouse in the centre of the city. Their home was now a modest garden apartment at the edge of town. Flip Zwarts was Jewish, his wife Joke was not – which we considered at this stage a definite advantage.* I was happy to come into this warm and cosy home that had a Christmas tree in the living room, shedding its needles but still twinkling with cheerful tinsel (it was early January), with people who knew me and my hidden past. Their daughter Elly, five years old, was sitting on her father's lap. Flip told her she was lucky to be here with a father and a mother, and nice food and toys, while there were other children who could not be with their parents. I felt tears welling up in my eyes. I

---

* Dutch Jews married to Gentiles were considered safe from deportation. But five months after my visit, Jewish partners of mixed marriages were given a terrible choice: submit to voluntary sterilization or be sent to a camp. The Zwartses all survived the war, although Flip did spend the last months of the war in Westerbork transit camp.

adored these people. I wished that I could stay there for ever and be their child.

Flip and Joke told me that 'Alfred' had been to see Father that morning.

'Jules!' I exclaimed. 'He's here?'

'He was here,' they said. 'As a matter of fact, he might stop by tomorrow morning, to pick up some things. He was hoping to bump into you.'

Sure enough, early the next morning my brother knocked on the door. 'Hey, Nettie!' he said as I strangled him in a big hug. 'Are you having a good time?'

Jules looked well, and very handsome in his cotton raincoat. It was lined, but I couldn't help worrying if he was warm enough in this cold and grizzly weather. He quickly told me that he had come to say goodbye to Father and get some money from him, because he was going to buy a boat that would take him to freedom. He had found a rusty old sloop in need of some minor repairs, but it would not take too much to make it sea-worthy. The plan was to transport the boat to Groningen, where Jules was on friendly terms with a reliable shipbuilder, and from there he would set off across the North Sea for England. Adrie was to go with him.

I was glad to see Jules so excited and full of confidence. There wasn't much time to talk. We both felt guilty about seeing each other; we were not supposed to be seen in the same place at the same time. It was foolishly risky. So we made it as short as possible. As we carried his bags downstairs, we speculated gaily about the future, when Jules would come home from England a war hero. I helped him load his bags on to his bicycle, and tucked his woollen scarf firmly around his neck. Jules got on his bike and, with one foot on the ground to keep himself and his luggage steady, he kissed me and whispered, 'See you very, very soon, Nettie. Remember, liberation is just around the corner.'

Jules, Miep and friends on Lake Kaag, 1942

Nina, Edith and Miep, 1942

Graduating class and faculty of the Jewish Lyceum, The Hague,
April 1942

The opening pages of Edith's third diary, showing a drawing of her by her
father, January 1941

9 Januari

Vanochtend heel vroeg op, om mijn
scheikunde repetitie te beëindigen. Ojé
hoe zal ik het gemaakt te hebben onmiddelijk
mmm maal gloofik. Vandaag was het
heel gezellig op school. Om 4 uur ben ik
gaan schaatsen hier op Arendsburg.
Met Hanne, Hilde en Mieke.
Het ijs worden de twee eersten zo
slecht, dat ze naar Clingendaal
zingen. wij bleven. Vanavond kwam
Jules weer opgewonden thuis
De maan schijnt vol, 't is heldere nacht
Zij zie in 't maandlicht engel wijzelfzen.
En spelen gitaar en... Ik wou er natuurlijk
dolgraag heen, maar mocht niet.
Moest mijn werk afmaken, heb gezellig
met Moeder, die m.C. op bed ligt, was
niet zo lekker.
Nu zal ik van mijn doen eens
moes naar bed gaan!

LEES DIT! Model No. 45 (Hsd.)
Bij briefwisseling met verpleegden en gevangenen moeten de naam en voornaam bovenaan IN DEN brief vermeld staan; op het adres mag de naam niet voorkomen.
Het adres is: AAN No. **92 - 13 29**.
GEVANGENIS
RIJKSWERKINRICHTING
Huis van Bewaring te Groningen

Ongefrankeerde brieven aan verpleegden en gevangenen worden niet aangenomen - POSTZEGELS en COUPONS mogen NIET worden toegezonden - De toezending van geld geschiedt per POSTWISSEL.

Groningen, 29 Jan. '43.

Mijn innig geliefde schat,
U zult wel niet aangenaam verrast zijn be-
richt van mij te krijgen uit de gevangenis. U dacht
mij zeker reeds lang in veiligheid? Helaas, het heeft
niet zo mogen zijn. Verleden Woensdag werd ik bij
iemand opgewacht, die ik meende te kunnen ver-
trouwen, en hier naar het Huis van Bewaring
gebracht. Gelukkig genoeg had ik juist te voren een
brief aan een vriend geschreven, en die ik nog niet gepost
had. U begrijpt welke verwijten ik mij gemaakt heb!
Maar buiten dat, had het zo moeten gebeuren.
het was nu eenmaal God's wil! Onvoorzichtig ben ik
gelukkig niet geweest. Mijn lieve schat, hoe is het
nu met U? Hoe deze brief U zal bereiken weet ik
niet, ik hoop in goede gezondheid. 6 maanden is
een lange tijd, en er heeft veel kunnen gebeuren...
Hoe is het nu met vadertje? O, schrijf toch eens
eens over jullie. Je begrijpt, dat ik brand van ver-
langen om iets te horen. Jammer dat ik in deze
omstandigheden moet horen, hoe het met jullie
gesteld is! Gelukkig ben ik nog zeer opgewekt en
optimistisch, mijn pech in aanmerking genomen

Above A page from the diary with an illustration by Edith of a skating scene, January 1941

Left The letter written by Jules from the House of Detention in Groningen, 1943

Guus after D-Day at the Siegfried Line near Aachen, December 1944

Paul van Hessen, Aunt Tine, Uncle Eb and Ineke zur Kleinsmiede with
Edith in the garden of no. 3 Cavaleriestraat, 1945

Uncle Eb, 1945

Dolf and Ineke at their engagement, 1947

Ineke and Dolf leaving for their civil wedding ceremony, spring 1950

Left Tine and her second husband, Job zur Kleinsmiede at Ineke's wedding, 1950

Below Loet and Edith with the twins, 1950

Aunt Tine and Edith at Yad Vashem, Jerusalem, where Aunt Tine
was made a 'Righteous Gentile', 1983

Aunt Tine and Edith at Yad Vashem during
the tree-planting ceremony, 1983

For the second time in six months I watched my brother wobble off, cheerfully waving with one hand as he manoeuvred his bike through the traffic.

Father had told everyone in the hospital that he was expecting a visit from the girlfriend of his son Guus, who was now in America.

On the way to the Department of Oral Surgery, I tried to steel myself for a shock. I knew from his and Mother's letters that the surgery had altered his appearance. Nothing could have prepared me, however, for the first sight of Father, the most wonderful, most invincible man in my life, now reduced to a vulnerable, frail figure sitting in a chair by the window. He had lost a lot of weight. His face was collapsed, almost unrecognizable. A ward assistant was hovering in the background.

'Mr van Hessen!' I exclaimed gaily. 'How good to see you!'

He got to his feet, and I saw that he was dressed in a neatly pressed grey suit. Aside from his drooping face, he was immaculate. 'Nettie, what a dear you are to come and see me. I know how busy you are, and it's so good of you to come to pay the old man a visit.' Even his voice was changed. The words were slurred, like an old man's; it was hard for him to articulate.

Taking my outstretched hands into his he called, 'Nurse! Come and meet my son's girlfriend, Nettie Schierboom. She has come all the way from Wassenaar to visit me. You remember my son Guus, the one I told you about who is in America? I bet she misses him even more than I do.' I smiled discreetly, hoping I looked like a slightly embarrassed girl who is being teased by her boyfriend's father. Then, politely, I started to ask him questions about his health.

He explained that the surgeon had had to remove his right jaw to stop the cancer from spreading. He praised the expertise of the surgeon, who was now waiting for the wound to heal so that a prosthesis could be fitted. I tried not to look, but my eyes kept being drawn back to that poor damaged face, horribly collapsed on one side.

Father got out his sketchbook to show me pictures he had drawn of his fellow patients, before and after their operations. Having become fascinated with the effects of the underlying bone structure on facial anatomy, he had been making a name for himself in the hospital as the in-house 'recorder'. Leafing through his sketchbook, I also found drawings and pastels of the hospital gardens as observed from his window or from a garden bench. It was moving to see how, in the confined space in which he now lived, he was constantly able to find new angles from which to perceive and draw his surroundings.

Finally the nurses left and we were alone for a few moments. I jumped up to get closer to him. We put our arms round each other and hugged. Father kissed me and whispered into my ear, 'Darling, I am so happy that you have come.'

'Doddeltje,' I choked, holding him tight. That was Mother's nickname for him. I did not dare call him 'Father'.

There was a clatter of footsteps in the corridor. Quickly I let go, and backed away to a respectful distance. 'Tell me, Mr van Hessen, how is Mrs van Hessen doing?' We resumed our polite small talk until there was another chance to steal a hug. As I sat there, I longed to touch him and grab his hand, to inhale his smell of tobacco and aftershave. But the stolen moments of intimacy were too short and too nerve-wracking.

A nurse brought him his lunch tray, and now I could see how ill he really was. He could not manage solid food and had to sip soup through a straw. The opening in his throat was not yet healed, and some soupy liquid spilled out of the wound. Father was embarrassed and told me to look the other way. 'You had better not look at me while I'm eating. It is not an attractive sight,' said this proper man whom I had never seen in his underwear, nor with a hair out of place. 'It doesn't matter!' I wanted to shout. 'I'll love you even if you make a mess of your food!' But the nurse had come back, and I sat quietly in my corner, smiling politely. We played our game perfectly. I didn't call him 'Father' and he didn't call me 'Edith' or 'Eetje'. We talked in code. He asked me how my 'dear parents' and Ineke were doing. He told me, as if in passing, that he had just received a visit from an old acquaintance – did I remember him, Alfred van Meurs? Ah yes, I responded vaguely. We did not discuss the boat, or Jules's plans. Soon it was time to leave – it would have looked suspicious had I stayed longer than the other visitors. I said goodbye to his nurses and the other patients I had met. Then Father courteously offered to accompany me to the gate, to 'show me the gardens, they really are quite lovely, even at this time of year'.

Outside, out of earshot, he told me again how much he loved me and how happy he was that I had found such a good home. He also said he was worried about Mother and that he missed her terribly. 'But have faith, child,' he added. 'Courage. I know you have lots of it. Always look for the sunshine.' At the gate, he took both my hands in his, and looked up at the hospital windows. 'I can't kiss you here, darling,' he said. 'But I am doing so in my mind.'

'Me too,' I said.

'The day will come,' said Father, his voice choked with emotion. 'The day will come.'

Slowly he turned round and returned to the hospital. He looked back once, and waved. As I stood there watching him disappear, I knew that I would never see him again.

17

Stranded

After visiting Father, there was nothing to do but return to Breda. Ineke and I had arranged to meet under the central clock at the train station. As I made my way through the crowds, I was jostled by a group of young German soldiers hurrying past. I felt the rough wool of their uniforms rub against my arm, and gazed straight ahead. I started noticing the people milling about, wondering if any of them were, like me, not who they were supposed to be. Or was I the only one? The only thing you could be sure of was that some of them were Nazi sympathizers – they would turn you in, given half a chance. But how could you tell which was which – who was good and who was bad?

To my great relief, there, under the clock, surrounded by shivering travellers, was Ineke, her calm pale eyes searching for me. My 'sister'. We fell on each other like long-lost friends. With Ineke at my side, I felt inconspicuous, safe. Two giggly girls on an outing. We found a compartment which was freezing cold, but empty. 'They'll turn on the heat once the train starts moving,' we told each other hopefully.

After two days, there was so much to tell. I filled Ineke in about my visit to Father, and I had just started telling her about 'Alfred' when three men in business suits entered our compartment, blowing into their cupped hands to warm their freezing fingers. They sat down without saying a word. Soon two of them were absorbed in their newspapers; the third sat staring out of the window with a tired, empty gaze and then nodded off. We kept our voices down, careful not to say anything that could give us away. We were both shivering, and huddled close to each other for warmth: the heat never came on.

After the second stop, as the train slowly moved out of the station, I noticed the sign Philips Gloeilampen Fabriek (Philips Light Bulb Factory). I wondered out loud why we had not seen the Philips factory on our way out. 'Maybe we were talking so much that we just didn't notice it,' said Ineke.

Then I jumped out of my seat. 'Philips! Philips is in Eind-hoven!' Eindhoven was due east of Breda. Anxiously we looked at our travelling companions. 'Is this the train for Breda?' we asked.

'No, you are on your way to Maastricht, I'm afraid,' said one of them, shaking his head. 'You should have changed trains at the first stop.'

The train was now moving at top speed. It was too late to get off. On the way to Utrecht we had been on the express train, and no one had informed us that we'd have to change trains on the return journey. 'There is only one thing to do,' the businessman said. 'You'll have to get off at the next stop, Weert, and take the first train back.'

It was six p.m. and it was getting dark. Anxiously we asked the conductor what to do, and he informed us, shaking his head, that our train would arrive in Weert too late to make the connection back to Utrecht that night, since all rail traffic stopped after the eight p.m. general curfew. We looked at each other in horror. What to do? We would have to be off the streets from eight until six the next morning. We didn't know a soul in Weert.

Ineke patted my hand as we tried to hide our consternation from our fellow passengers. My mind was racing, but I told myself to remain calm. In silence, we stared out at the dusky meadows racing by with dark clusters of cows huddled together against the cold. Now and then we would catch each other's eyes in the reflection in the window.

I went over the options, one by one. No good going to the police for help, of course. The same went for a hotel or inn: at the reception desk, we would be asked to show our identity papers. More likely than not these would then be taken to the police station or Gestapo headquarters to be checked. Every person who stayed away from his place of residence for longer than twenty-four hours was supposed to register with the police in the town he or she was visiting. I knew the Germans had a registry of lost or stolen identity cards – it was easy for them to catch 'illegals' like myself.

By the time we got off the train, we had less than an hour to find a solution. Who would take us in? We did not have enough money to bribe someone; besides, how would we know whom to trust?

Walking from the station into the centre of town, we quickly decided on a story. Two sisters, from a poor family, we were on our way back from visiting our grandfather in Utrecht but we had boarded the wrong train and now found ourselves stranded with no money for a hotel. 'But where shall we go?' moaned Ineke.

An inspiration came to me. 'A doctor or a priest. Human lives are important to them. If we can't trust one of them, we can't trust anyone.' Ineke thought that was a good idea. It was now 7.30, half an hour until curfew.

We found ourselves on a quiet street. The houses were all dark, because of the blackout. We imagined families safely gathered round the dinner table behind their heavy curtains or black blinds, eating their supper by lamplight and the shimmering of a Christmas tree. A young woman was hurrying towards us carrying a child on her hip. We decided we'd risk it. After all, she looked sympathetic and she had a child. How could she be bad? 'Excuse us,' we asked politely, 'but could you please tell us where we could find a doctor or a priest?' Hurriedly we told her the story we'd made up. 'So you see,' we said, 'we have to get off the street somehow. We were hoping to find someone who would let us into their garden or shed, just for tonight.'

'You're in luck, girls,' the young woman said. 'You happen to be standing right in front of the vicarage. Father Josephus lives here. Try him.' Then she hurried on, explaining she'd be late for curfew.

The vicarage was a tall, white, elegant old townhouse. There was not a chink of light to show if anyone was home. We pulled the heavy brass bell by the side of the door. We waited a long time. We heard no sound inside. We rang the bell again, more urgently this time. I was beginning to lose hope.

Then, suddenly, we heard a scratching at the doorknob. I thought my heart would be crushed in my chest, it was beating so hard. This was perhaps the scariest moment of my life – but it was also exciting. My life had suddenly turned into an adventure!

An old woman opened the door. After we stammered out our story, she opened the door all the way and told us to enter. 'Wait in the hall,' she said, 'and I'll tell Pater Josephus that he has visitors.' After a long miserable wait, a middle-aged man in a dressing-gown and slippers came down the stairs. I decided he had a kind and open face. He acted as if our plea to be allowed to spend the night in his garden or shed was the most normal request in the world.

'No, no,' he said, 'just come in! You don't have to stay out in the garden. Here, come into the parlour, where it's nice and warm. Pull a chair up to the fire and relax.' He told his housekeeper to bring us some food, which we fell on ravenously. Then he sat with us a while, talking about literature, philosophy and other neutral subjects. He never once asked us a personal question about ourselves.

Eventually he excused himself, but not before making sure that his housekeeper had brought us everything we needed for the night – pillows, blankets and a footstool, so that we could rest comfortably in our chairs by the fire. We fell asleep at once, grateful to be indoors, out of the dark January night.

At five a.m. the housekeeper woke us with a cup of hot coffee (made with real coffee beans!), farmer's bread, fresh butter and home-made jam. We splashed some cold water on our faces, then ate our delicious breakfast and thanked our host profusely. Father Josephus walked us to the door and handed us a package containing fresh bacon, butter, eggs and a loaf of bread hot from the oven. 'For your parents,' he said. 'Because they must have had a pretty unpleasant night, not knowing where you were. Please don't thank me. Just catch your train and get home safe, do you hear? God bless you, girls.'

After the war I sent a letter with a little gift to Pater Josephus in the town of Weert, thanking him for saving my life. The package came back stamped 'Addressee unknown'. I tried to find out what had happened to him, but no one could tell me where he had gone. Much later I discovered that Pater Josephus had been in the Resistance and, like many other priests, had been caught and executed.

18

Jules

Soon after my visit to Father, Mrs z.K. took the train to The Hague to visit Mother in hospital. She brought her a letter from me describing my visit in detail. Mother wrote back:

My dearest beloved friend,
What a surprise yesterday when your mother [Mrs z.K.] suddenly stood by my bed. We embraced, and immediately started calling each other by our first names. She was a ray of light in the darkness of my loneliness. Your letter was like a screenplay – I lived it all with you so intensely; I reread your letter at least ten times. Jealous is not the right word, but how I would have given up everything that's dear to me to have held you in my arms too. Like a dog panting on a hot summer day – how I yearned for you when I heard your stories.
Your grandmother sent me a letter in which she says she isn't very happy in Amsterdam. I write three times a week and send her food coupons, because she is not getting much to eat there. I do as much as I can for her. The inscription on my own grandmother's gravestone read, 'Her life consisted of lovingly taking care of others'. I wonder, will those be the words on my tombstone too, a hundred years from now? Oh, what a gloomy way to talk! Because I have to tell you I am really in a very good mood, darling, and expect better days to come. They *will* come, I am sure of it.

I still can't walk very well; everyone jumps out of the way when they see me coming. Still, I know that some day I'll go swimming again with you, at the lake. But then there had better be some steps or a ladder so I can climb back into the boat. Remember the last time, when I had such a struggle to get back in? I won't let you kids make fun of me again.

Here nobody goes out any more. Everyone just vegetates. Even the nurses, when you ask them, 'What are your plans for tonight?' answer: 'Oh nothing, I'm staying in with a book.' So – you aren't missing anything, child. You say that you've gained weight – well, that's a good sign, at least you have enough to eat. It doesn't matter. Soon, we will do our exercises together again. None of your friends are left. The twins Polly and Dolly have joined Renée.*

Mrs z.K. reported that Mother was now able to stand up, and was encouraged to make short and painful excursions down the hospital corridor, leaning on a walker. She was trying to get Father moved to her own hospital, but his doctors insisted that he remain where he was for more surgery and radiation therapy.

I was haunted by the picture of my two parents – my graceful mother crippled by a broken hip, my father's handsome face devastated by a diseased jaw. What was it about bones, I wondered, that could leave you so horribly vulnerable? I took my mother's advice to heart, and embarked on a stringent exercise regime. I was not going to let myself go soft and flabby. I would make myself strong and muscular, like my brother Jules. Even though he and I did not write to each other, I had news of him via Miep, who was more in love with him than ever. In January she had a typically light-hearted, bantering letter from him:

---

* i.e. deported to Poland.

Utrecht, 17 January '43
My dear little Miep,

My affairs are going terrifically well. This is not a good-bye letter yet (of course not, if it was it would be bathed in tears!) because I was hoping to come and say goodbye in person one evening before taking the last train back. Will you write so we can work it out?

Miep, you know you are my best friend, I wear your monkey good-luck charm faithfully, close to my heart, so how can anything bad happen to me? I'll still be seeing you, in any case. Please give my regards to all the family. A loving kiss.

Your friend,
Alf

Then, the unthinkable. It is hard for me to express, even now, what I felt when Adrie wordlessly pressed an envelope into my hand one black day in February. There were two letters, one from Mother, the other one a scribbled note, in Jules's bold handwriting, on a piece of prison notepaper. It was addressed to Mother.

House of Detention, Groningen, 29 January 1943
Dearest, most beloved one,

You will not be happily surprised to hear from me from jail. You thought I had long reached safety? Alas, it isn't so. Last Wednesday, at the home of someone I thought I could trust, they were waiting for me and brought me to the House of Detention. Unfortunately, I had just written a letter to a friend and had not yet had time to post it. You can understand how angry I was with myself. Besides that, perhaps it was meant to happen like this, it is God's will, after all. I hadn't taken any risks – honest!

My dear love, how are you now? I hope in good health. Six months is a long time. How is Father now? Please write how you are. You can understand that I am burning to hear something, although I am sorry it is under these circumstances. Considering my bad luck, I am still quite cheerful and optimistic. The first days I was pretty depressed. But I have accepted my fate and will make the best of it. Our fate lies in God's hands and I am sure He will pull us through. Mother dear, you have always had confidence in me: I will not let you down. I know I can weather even this storm.

My cellmate is a very pleasant fellow. They're treating us all right. The prison guards are friendly people and the food is sufficient. I have no complaints so far. Next week they will probably send us to Westerbork* and from there they'll move us on. I'm full of courage, and am keeping my head high. Naturally, I have nothing with me and I probably will not be able to recover my clothes, which are still in Utrecht. Would it be possible for you to send me some underwear, overalls, a pair of old shoes, some socks, some pants and a shirt? If you do it soon, it will probably still get here in time. Some money would be nice, too (by money-order). Twenty guilders would be fine.

Write me back soon, dearest, because I'm only allowed to write two letters a month, but there are no restrictions on how many I can receive. (For safety's sake, they should come only from you.) I hug you and pray that we'll see each other again soon.

Your loving son,

Jules

PS. I'll try to look up cousin Otto when I am in Westerbork. How is Eetje, and her friend? Please write about them

---

* Westerbork was a concentration camp situated inside the Netherlands with a direct rail link to Auschwitz, Sobibor and the other extermination camps.

especially. Give everyone my love and please send me what I need as soon as possible – also some toiletries . . . and pyjamas?

I quickly scanned Mother's accompanying letter for a hint of who it was who could have betrayed Jules, but I found none. In her distraught state Mother was more reckless than she had ever been in her letters to me, totally forgetting to write in code.

My beloved daughter, my darling, my Moeschele, my everything!

Finally I have a chance to write to you again. It causes me such agony that I cannot have news from you on a more regular basis. But even that one has to accept, if one doesn't want to lose one's mind. These last weeks your thoughts and words have given me such strength. I sensed that you were really tuned into Father and me.

You see, my instinct told me that something terrible had happened to one of my loved ones. Telepathy definitely exists – I had a feeling. Even though I did not yet know *what* had happened, and to which one of you, I had a foreboding, in my heart and in my head. It was so strong that on the day that Jules was arrested (. . . oh but that thought makes me go crazy . . . my child, whom I carried so tenderly under my heart!) I had had a long talk with Miep, and told her it would be better for her not to be so in love with Jules, not to count too much on him, because Jules is single, unattached, and that's better for now. I didn't want her to be disappointed later. I told her to regard it as a true friendship and the rest will come later. I was restless all that day, and also the next, when Miep's mother came to visit me. I said, 'I have such a strange feeling that something has happened to my husband or my children or my mother.' 'Come,' she said, 'you worry too much!' I couldn't sleep that night, nor the next. Early the following morning, I called their house. I was so upset I couldn't speak and asked Uncle Lex to come and see me as soon as he could. He came around twelve. 'Out with it,' I said. 'I know something is up. Tell me.'

'Jules has been arrested,' was his reply.

I had been prepared for something like this, but still it felt as if I was sinking through the floor.

When I was done weeping, I immediately began to contact my circle of friends who might have some influence with the authorities. I received a long letter from Jules in prison that I want you to read: very cheerful and courageous. He is not allowed any visitors, only a lawyer. My tears blinded me: I could hardly finish the letter. He was betrayed by someone, and now he'll be sent to Westerbork. I got out of bed and called the best lawyer I know, and also your Mr Keyser, who immediately sent someone to see me. They are going to send Jules the clothing he has asked for. When the lawyer came I showed him the letter from Hitler,* and I also told him about my own nursing work for Germany during the last war. That should help Jules. God grant that he is not sent on, that he remains alive. That is my greatest worry. Everybody has been praying for him. The chaplain here too. They wanted to keep it a secret from me at first, but what good would that have done? I would have pulled all my hair out if I had been stopped from doing what I can for my Jules. At least now he can have as many letters from me as he is allowed to receive, and packages.

I read your lovely letter to Paps before it went to him. It moved me, as always. How I miss you, Moeschele! Your picture is next to my bed and I often talk to you. I can hear

---

* The document showing that Omi had sacrificed a son for the Fatherland.

your voice: 'Mother dear, just keep going, we'll soon be together again!' I want to feel your hand on my forehead. Tomorrow will be the thirtieth Sunday since you and Jules left me, and now he is in the hands of those wicked, wicked scoundrels. I saw it coming. He wasn't careful enough, he took a lot of risks. Or would it have happened anyway?

Aat has to hide too. It's a madhouse here. Everybody is being rounded up. I don't know how many thousands of people. There's a rumour that girls are getting picked up too. But that may just be the girls who were arrested for laughing during the funeral of SS General Seyffardt.* Still, Miep and Nina don't go out any more; no one comes to see me, everyone stays home.

Poor Omi misses everyone so much. I write to her three times a week. I don't want her to know about Jules. See how I have to pretend! My biggest worry is our dear Doddel. I write to him every day. His health in tatters, and no one to confide in. His last operation was no little thing. They took out his lymph gland and gave him radiation treatment for two weeks (the kind Madame Curie wrote about), which made him terribly nauseous. Today is the last day of the treatment. There is so much for us to bear. If only I could be sure that everything would turn out all right in the end, I should be glad to carry the weight of these troubles on my shoulder. Remember the proverb: 'Carry your burden, and do not complain.'

Lex [Miep's father] just stopped by. He can't visit as often as he used to, but I do see him once a week. They have their own troubles now, like everyone else. Their niece

* General Seyffardt, a Dutch general who had gone over to the Waffen-SS, was assassinated in early February 1943 by members of the Resistance. Hecklers at his funeral were hauled off to prison. Mother was trying to warn me that if non-Jewish girls were now being rounded up as well, I was doubly at risk.

Fietje, whose husband was a doctor at the mental institution at Apeldoorn, has been sent to Westerbork. Apparently all the mental patients are already on their way to Germany or Poland, with their nurses and doctors.* How lucky I am that you at least are where you are!

I read something this week that made a deep impression on me. Listen to it, darling: 'What is important is not what function we are assigned to in life. What matters is how we accomplish the task.' Though your life may seem tedious and boring to you now, be happy that you are staying with such good people, and perform your task well. Everybody is suffering these days. We have to pull through. We must! Do you hear me, darling? Because only the strong will get the chance to help rebuild a new society.

Adrie told me he would have to stop visiting us for a while. Since Jules had had an incriminating letter on him at the time of his arrest, it was best for him to lie low. Besides, more and more young men, Jewish or not, were being picked up for the labour camps. Adrie was crushed about Jules's arrest: his hopes for escape were in ruins.

It was only a matter of days before Mother heard that Jules had been put on a transport for Poland.

It's Sunday morning. Yesterday I received the terrible news. Jules has been sent on.† Dear angel, you will understand

---

* Eleven hundred Jewish mental patients, together with the medical staff who had volunteered to accompany them, were put on a special train that went straight to the gas chambers at Auschwitz.

† After the war, a cousin who had been at Westerbork at the same time as Jules explained why Jules was sent on to Poland so quickly. Jules had made two escape attempts, whether from prison, during his transfer to the prison camp, or while at Westerbork, I am not sure. This meant my brother had two strikes against him. He was labelled with the dreaded 'S', which meant that he was earmarked for special punishment.

my feelings. I thought I would sink through the floor. I suffered a terrible shock to my nerves but I am over it now. I cried all night long, but what good will that do? The only thing that helps is faith that he will return. He is strong, and that gives me hope. All my efforts on his behalf were useless. My poor Jules! You will understand, darling, how my heart bleeds! I thought I would go mad, but then Uncle Lex came, and stayed with me for over two hours. First I had to sacrifice my brother to these criminals, and now they have taken my son! A mere boy, who never did anything wrong . . . May God the Almighty keep him whole and able to withstand everything. It is a harsh trial, for me as well as for him, but I believe in God, that He is *with me*. My most fervent wish is that nothing happens to you, child.

I don't want Daddy to know about Jules's deportation just yet. His mood is so low in any case, and he won't find out, because I was the one who was writing to him. My last letter was returned, stamped 'Return to sender' and 'On Transport'. Then I knew. Now you know too: let Father get better first, there is time enough to tell him. I wish I could cut myself into pieces: one half for him and the other half to be divided among you and Jules and our poor Guus. What on earth must Guus think when he hears the stories about his homeland! And his fears for his loved ones . . . Yesterday the chaplain comforted me, and he has promised to pray for our Jules, the child I carried under my heart, gave birth to and brought up with so much love . . . Oh, it's enough to make you lose your mind . . .

I just learned that it was a large transport. Dentists, other professionals, large families, all gone. I hope he can stay tough. Besides, they can't possibly all be killed. There are so many German prisoners of war being held by the Allies. Surely they'll think twice before they kill all these people, because if they do, their own people might be treated the same way. I put my trust in God. He will protect us.

And you, my darling? Do you still have courage? Can you take your mother as your example? One can live without pleasure, but one cannot live without *hope*. I resist the black thoughts as much as I can. Be glad that you have work to do, because that is what I myself miss most. I once read somewhere, 'Only through work can man realize his own worth.' What do you think about all those boys who have been rounded up? Aat is safe, don't worry about him. I miss him too, because he was one of my most faithful visitors. He and his family have shown me what friendship is really about.

Whoever betrayed Jules in Groningen has got something coming! When Jules gets back he will be able to tell us exactly what happened. How cheerful he sounded, in prison. If only we had gone to America when we still had the chance!

Yesterday Mr Keyser came here in person for the first time, but he cannot do anything for Jules. His little sister has not been deported yet. He has a top post on the Jewish Council. Do you have enough underwear and clothes? Buy whatever you need. And surprise Mrs z.K. every now and then with a little gift. Never forget your upbringing and the love which you must now pass on to others.

Your loving, true Mother

PS. You must NOT keep my letters. After you have read them, burn them.

In her next letter, Mother reported that every letter she had sent to Jules had been returned. Miep's heart was broken; she had taken to her bed, and was very sick. The raw grief that Mother was sharing with me now was something new and terrible, yet I think in her own way she was trying to teach me a lesson in coping. She showed me that no matter how deep the wound, you could ease the pain by remembering the good times.

My darling love, my only consolation,
This morning I got back all the letters that I had sent to Jules . . . and the bandage over my great wound was ripped off again. But what can you do? Only have faith that he will return to us. Whenever I eat or go to sleep, I think: 'What does he have to still his hunger? And what does he have to shield him against the cold?' Child, I will not and cannot have those thoughts, otherwise I shall never survive this. I must pull myself together. I tell myself it will all soon be over. Didn't I do the right thing three years ago to send Guus away? That was 1 March 1940, I remember it as if it were yesterday. If only I had sent Jules too! If only, if only – that's no way to think. So – I think about happy things, or at least I *try* to. I think about the time when you were all still home with me. Remember, darling, our wonderful Friday nights, or that St Nicolaas night when I dressed up as the good saint? And when we were moving to the house in Scheveningen and I crashed through the bedroom floor, remember? And when we two set out for Sinsheim very early in the morning, so the boys wouldn't notice us leaving? What wonderful times we had, the summer months at the lake . . . the little house where you slept in bunk-beds . . . that is my salvation, my memories, otherwise I could not bear it.

Mother could not keep the news of Jules's deportation from Father for very long. He could not bring himself to write about it to me, but he found relief in attending to practical matters – our financial situation, for instance. He decided it would be best to sell Jules's boat, and asked Adrie to take care of it for him. Adrie, who was devastated not only by his friend's arrest but also by the fact that without Jules he saw his own chances of escape go up in smoke, arranged to have the boat moved to a lake near Loosdrecht, where he knew a shipbuilder interested in buying it.

In the late spring Adrie wrote me a letter describing in glowing terms his sailing trip in Jules's boat from Groningen to Loosdrecht. He had asked a group of friends to come along, and they had spent a weekend on the lake before turning the boat over to the shipbuilder. He wrote that the weekend had been a lot of fun.

A lot of fun! In poor Jules's boat! Something snapped in me. I could no longer play the good sport. How could Adrie be so insensitive? This marked a turning point in my feelings for Adrie, although it was to take several more months before I could admit to myself what I had been feeling for some time: that our values were different.

I never did find out at whose house it was that the Gestapo had been lying in wait for Jules, or which 'friend' had turned him in. After the war, I did make some enquiries, but everyone in Groningen who had known him swore how they had helped him, how fond they had been of him, what a wonderful boy he was. I had my suspicions. But I never could prove a thing. In any case, the thought of revenge gradually faded from my mind. It was Adolf Hitler, after all, who was the ultimate culprit. Jules's fate was sealed. There was nothing anyone could have done to save him.

Less than a month later Mother was lifted from her hospital bed at three a.m. and sent to Westerbork.

19

Mother

During the early months of 1943, the Sicherheitspolizei,* striking in the middle of the night, stormed every hospital in the country and emptied the wards of Jewish patients, no matter how ill. On 5 March it was the turn of The Hague's Municipal and Roman Catholic hospitals. By the time the local populace woke up the next morning and heard about the round-up, it was too late to do anything about it. Hundreds of Jewish patients had been neatly 'transferred' to the sick bays of Camp Westerbork.

For some unknown reason, Father was left behind in Utrecht. Why he was not taken was a mystery. He had already made it abundantly clear that if 'they' came for him, he would not go. He was too sick, and had told his doctors that his choice was to die instead. In early April he received a notice that he had to report to Vught concentration camp (not far from Breda) by the twenty-third of that month, but he ignored the order. No one knows if it was the hospital management who protected him or if the doctors were able to claim that they needed Father to complete a medical experiment. Perhaps it was simply a bureaucratic oversight; but Father remained where he was.

Westerbork, where Mother had been taken, was the main transit camp in Holland for Jews destined for the crematoria

* Security Police.

of Auschwitz–Birkenau and Sobibor. It was situated in a bleak and isolated spot in the eastern part of Holland, close to the German border. It had all the hallmarks of a concentration camp – the mud, the overcrowded barracks, watch towers, barbed wire, railway sidings. The people who arrived there lived in harsh conditions, but they were permitted to receive a limited amount of mail and parcels, and they were able to report back to their friends and family that it was, generally, bearable. Disease was rampant, but the sick were well cared for in the camp hospital; the prisoners were permitted to celebrate the Jewish holidays; there was an orchestra, a school and even a theatre-cabaret featuring talented performers. It was felt that if you remained in Westerbork and were not 'sent on', you might be all right.

Mother remained at Westerbork for two months. Confined to bed in the infirmary at first, she was later, when her leg started to mend, assigned to some menial jobs. She came across several friends and relatives there, and was able to find out what had happened to many others who had disappeared. She wrote as often as she could to Father (two letters a month were permitted). Father would copy each precious letter and send it on to me via my messengers.

Westerbork, 12 March 1943
My beloved darlings,

I look forward for days to the moment that I am permitted to write to you. That is the only thing I have not grown used to: so little communication with my loved ones. Your letters are the 'Eldorado' for me – to hear that you are well is an elixir of life.

I have grown used to things here. I am luckily pretty adaptable. The first weeks are difficult here for everyone, but those who are able to forget the past and keep their nerves in check, can at least make themselves useful to the others. I know how to get by and my immense will-power is of great value to me now.

Our barrack houses 115 women, both old and young. I have found many friends among them who are very kind and concerned. But the faces change all the time – people come and go. Frieda [a sister-in-law] left on the last transport. I managed to send her a parcel via her niece who is here too but I didn't get to see her because I couldn't walk that far. I learned that your brother Julius* is arriving today. That completes our family.

My darling, how is the radiation working? It's like a bad dream, all of this, and the fact that I can do so little for you is the worst. Omi, I can understand your sorrow, but please don't worry so much – spring is on the way and the cold winter has passed. I received the warm clothes that Jetty [Fernandes] sent me; they are *indispensable* in this place. If you hear of anybody else who has to leave, advise him or her to pack wisely. No unnecessary items, and no suitcases. Let them put all their belongings in rucksacks. Fortunately I now have everything under control – I arrived here with only my slippers!

Whether my nursing work during the last war will have any influence on my case is doubtful, but the documents you sent me will be useful for Omi at any rate. Visiting hours in the infirmary here are from 4.30 to 5.00. It gets so crowded that nobody gets anything out of the visit. Dr Kam, Tobias, Marion Buchsbaum and her husband, your cousin Karel, Miss Kanner, the Zimmerns, Sanders, Krakauers, Miss Mannheimer, the niece of Erna Mayer-Wolf . . . too many to list, have all come by to visit. Here there is no radium left. I hope you will first get better my darling and then you can join me later.

* My uncle, not my brother.

It wasn't long before Omi, too, was unceremoniously taken from the Jewish Invalide in Amsterdam and dumped at Westerbork. To make matters worse, Omi's rucksack had been mixed up with someone else's, and instead of having her own things, she had to make do with an old man's clothes. Now that Mother had someone else to worry about, she was motivated to get up and about as soon as possible, because, she wrote, 'One *has* to be healthy here!'

What a shock I had when I discovered Omi among the latest arrivals here! The poor soul has had a terrible time. The second day after she arrived she fell ill. Diarrhoea – the most common camp sickness. Now she is lying in the bed next to mine with influenza. You can understand that this definitely is not making my life any easier, but the dear Lord will give me the strength I need to withstand it all.

Every day I hope for the arrival of the papers that I need. You, darling, really have to push harder to hasten the process. Also, do everything you can to get yourself on the 'Frederiks List' with family (this is what your cousin Karel van Hessen advised).*

I have to report with great sadness that your brother Julius and his wife Henny have been sent on. Julius was very brave. Cousin Otto tried everything possible, but to no avail. Jette and Olga are also gone, and many, many more. God preserve them. Who is next? I just received a statement from the Jewish Council – that I was never a member. So that's that. But the certificates of baptism from Reverend Niewenhuis (or whatever his name is) for myself

---

* A list named after a Dutch bureaucrat that supposedly exempted from deportation those who were on it.

and Omi have not yet arrived.* I know you can't get back into our house, but perhaps someone can obtain a duplicate of my brother's death certificate?

Darling, you *know* that I think of you day and night, don't you? For what is my life without you? And still I find the strength every day to be a support for Omi and our other friends here. Sometimes I don't understand it myself. But then I think it is all because of my conviction and my hope to return to what was dear to me. Omi has aged tremendously. It was a shock when I first saw her. She is very depressed and also somewhat confused. Will you write to me often? It's the only thing I really want. I've had some letters, from Marie and Dop and also from Nettie, and that makes me want to go on living, all those dear friends. Give them all my love. I cannot write to them individually, to thank them. Explain it to them. But don't let them forget me! Life in de Mildestraat was so much more fun. Will I live to see our house again?

The tone of Mother's letters became increasingly desperate as she sought a release for herself and Omi before the inevitable order to board a cattle-truck for the east came through. I knew that Father was doing everything in his power to persuade people with influence to help. I myself felt strangely calm, frozen in utter helplessness.

Often I considered what would happen if I just gave myself up. I was longing to be sent to Westerbork, where at least I

---

* Rumour had it that a release might be obtained if you were in possession of certain documents, such as a statement saying that you had never been a member of any Jewish congregation. Mother had also been trying to obtain bogus certificates of baptism from a friendly minister, since in July 1942 the Dutch Reformed Church had received an assurance from the *Reichkommissar* that any Jew who had been baptized in the church prior to 1941 would be exempted from deportation. (This promise, like so many others, proved worthless in the end.) Mother's other attempts at finding a way out focused on the sacrifices she and Omi had made for Germany in the First World War.

would be with my own people. I wanted to help Mother and Omi. I missed them so terribly. I was strong, I could work, I could help the others, take care of them. After all, how terrible could it be over there? Surely no worse than this stifling existence, where I felt dead inside, a non-person skulking behind my adopted family. The trouble was that in giving myself up, I would betray the z.K.s too. So even that was not an option. No, the only thing I could do was write, write, as many letters as possible, to try to keep up my parents' flagging spirits.

Westerbork, 9 April 1943
My dear husband,

Your letters, darling . . . are my life-line. Write to me often or send me a telegram when there's something important. This is no time to sleep. You have enough friends who would do anything for you, as long as you take the initiative. Perhaps the fact that your father was a member of the Groningen City Council could be helpful to Lex in his efforts on your behalf? So you see I keep hoping for a way out of here every day. Did you ask for the papers I need? If only we had taken care of these things sooner! . . . I hope the papers you sent me will do Omi some good. Perhaps you'll still ask my friend in the hospital if he can retrieve that '*Angehörigkeitsbescheinigung*'* from our house? Any news from Groningen? You must not rest until you have collected all the papers. I am sorry for all the trouble, but it has to be done.

Darling, do you sense how often I think of you and the others? The days pass by and my heart is sad . . . Sometimes I think, how can one bear this? Your letters perform wonders, and your love makes me strong. I walk much better now, except that I am still in some pain.

---

* Certificate of affiliation – probably a veiled reference to the faked baptismal certificate.

Please thank all our friends for their relief parcels. Isn't it wonderful to have such friends? I have found someone here, too, who is just like a sister to me; with selfless devotion she has been helping me care for Mother. The people are so kind. The matron here is very good to me and I give her a hand when I can. I can use everything; we still need warm underwear. Ask Jetty to send one or two warm nightgowns and trousers – Omi has nothing. I also desperately need my dressing-gown, I've asked Jetty for it four or five times. Why hasn't she sent it yet? I'm freezing here! Omi's rucksack was lost, she has an old man's clothes, so you understand how thankful we are for warm clothes. Will you make sure the things are inspected first and treated for moths? Otherwise they are of no use . . .

It makes me feel good that you have such a steady correspondence with our little friend. She is often on my mind. Tell her how much I love her and that I am proud to have her love and her respect. Where do you think Budi* is now? Is our guardian angel watching over him? Omi does not know he has been deported.

Finally, a letter came from Mother written specially for me. I appreciated her honesty: I felt that she was finally treating me as an adult. She wrote that she had received a card from Jules, saying he was 'well'; he was in Birkenau, a place we had never heard of.† That in itself did not sound too ominous, although it did seem very far away.

---

* Jules.

† The Jewish Council reported in December 1942 that eighty-three letters and eighteen postcards had been received from Auschwitz–Birkenau, all stating the same thing: that the correspondent was in relatively good shape, that they were working in the 'fresh air' and that food and care was 'satisfactory'. Families were told that they could write to their relatives in the camps. Thousands of letters were gathered by the Jewish Council and handed over to the authorities. The letters were never delivered: the Nazis destroyed them all.

Westerbork, 7 May 1943
My dearest friend,

You must have wondered, darling, why there was no sign of life from me in such a long time. Yet I'm sure you sensed that I am with you, always! Sweetheart, you know that my dear husband is very ill and I must comfort him as best I can in the few letters that are permitted to me here. But today I want to chat with you, Moeschele, because my heart is heavy, and I feel like pouring it out to you, like a child to its mother. My dear husband is alone, far from everyone he loves, suffering pain, always more pain, sometimes unbearable . . . How cruel it is that I cannot help him in any way. I worry about him day and night and wonder what he has done to deserve such suffering. You know our family, and so I know you feel what I am going through. Do please write to my husband often, and give him all your courage and your strength, so that he will make it through. May God Almighty stand by him and give him some measure of light and happiness still. Sometimes it is as if everything around me has gone dark. But just a moment ago I had a lovely surprise: I received your letter, my dear friend.

Well! For a moment it brought me back into an old-fashioned jolly mood. But my worry about my beloved husband will not let me rest. I cannot paint a picture in words of the state of my soul. But I promise you one thing, darling, that I'll stay strong no matter what happens. For I want to survive.

The news from Budi made me so happy. I hope that he remains well. Did you write to him yet? He will be so happy to hear from us.

My life is like a valuable vase that has been broken, and I am trying to gather up all the bits and pieces and glue them all together again. Omi, fortunately, is doing a little better. The pneumonia and fever have made her weak. She clings to her memories for moments of happiness. All she talks about is Guus and his brother and little sister – you know.

I myself am much improved, I can walk now, without crutches, and can handle small tasks in the infirmary. When I work, my worries are momentarily forgotten and time passes more quickly. Did you receive Doddel's drawing? I would like to hear more about your family in Breda; give them my best wishes, especially your sister. She will have taken her exams by now. If I had had the opportunity of sending her a little gift, I would surely have done so.

I would give anything to be allowed to sit next to you, quietly, with your hand in mine, understanding each other . . . Perhaps the day will still come. But remember that I'll always remain the same person I have always been! It's too bad that I cannot write a book about all of this while I'm in here.

Dearest Moeschele, I wrap you in my arms and give you a big hug. Stay healthy and write soon. Could someone send me a piece of soap?

With deep love I kiss you, (Omi too),

Your old faithful friend

PS. I need hairpins and toothpaste.

The zur Kleinsmiedes were always respectfully discreet when I received letters via our couriers, and let me retire to my attic room to digest whatever tidings they contained. But, as my parents kept repeating over and over, my family's tragedy was nothing special; everyone was suffering, and I felt it my duty not to taint the atmosphere by letting it get me down.

Even though the news they carried was never good, I always found myself looking forward to a visit from Adrie's parents. Uncle Aa was a charming man, warm and full of jokes, and

Aunt Dop was a sweet, sensitive soul with considerable insight into my predicament. So when at the end of May Mrs z.K. announced, after reading the morning's mail, that the 'visitors' were coming, my heart leapt: perhaps this time they would have something hopeful to tell us.

Mrs z.K. went down to the cellar to fetch an armload of special treats: a tin of sardines, some eggs preserved in aspic (the pickled eggs were kept in a large ceramic pot with a heavy lid on a cellar rack) and a jar of redcurrant jelly. Delicacies like these were served only on very special occasions. Mrs z.K. was a very careful hoarder, and stretched her precious stores in a mysterious fashion, understood only by her, that was intended to make them last until the day we were liberated. How Ineke and I wished that she would throw all caution to the wind just once, and say, 'Oh, the hell with it, let's splurge!' But that was not Mrs z.K.'s way.

The Verhulsts arrived late, and, after gorging ourselves, we all went straight to bed. The next morning, after breakfast, the four adults decided to stroll into town for a cup of 'coffee' (brewed from roasted chicory, since coffee beans were no longer to be had) at a terrace near the marketplace. There was no question of my going along: besides my visits to the grocer's and the bakery, I never ventured into town now. Ineke was at school. It was Tuesday, my day for cleaning the master bedroom and study. The adults' apologetic goodbyes still ringing in my ears, I went upstairs, whistling, with my duster and vacuum cleaner. I kicked myself for forgetting to ask Aunt Dop if she had a letter for me from Father, or a copy of one of Mother's letters from Westerbork.

I made the beds and, humming 'Moonlight and Shadows', started slapping my duster carelessly over the mahogany dressing table and chest, scattering dust in all directions. As I came to the bedside table next to Mrs z.K.'s bed, an envelope with Mother's familiar handwriting caught my eye. Puzzled,

I wondered what Mother's letter was doing here, in the z.K.s' bedroom. Had they found my secret cache of undestroyed letters? If they had, I was in trouble!

My foster parents' strong Calvinistic beliefs (held despite the fact that they were not churchgoers and called themselves atheists) had been rubbing off on me, and I knew that it was wrong to snoop, to read something not intended for my eyes. But this was different. This letter could not possibly be for anyone but me. What was it doing there?

Suddenly it hit me, like a bullet between the eyes. The messengers had come again. To give me this letter. They simply had not had the courage to do it yet. It must contain some very bad news. They had gone out to discuss with the z.K.s the best way to break it to me.

Shaking, I reached for the envelope and pulled out Mother's letter. It was addressed to Father.

Westerbork, 23 May 1943
Darling,

I love you with all my heart and beg you not to give up the fight. I will definitely return and then we'll resume the life we created together with our children, long before this nightmare began. You must do everything you can to get better because when I get back, I will need you more than ever. I want you to fight off this illness and not let yourself be bowed down by the cruelties the Nazis are inflicting on us. I need you when I come back! I need you to *be* there!

Tell my little friend that she is lucky. She must continue to do her duty, and much more, for those wonderful people who have done so much for us. Tell her I am proud of her, that I love her and will come back soon.

Tonight I go on transport. Omi and I are on the list. Omi is very ill and suffers greatly. She has grown weak and very old. I now walk with a stick and will probably be able to work there. Will do my best. You both do your best too, do you hear? I count on you and will need you when I return. You HAVE to be there!

Love you for ever,
Hilde

The letter fell back on to the bedside table. I looked up at the ceiling which badly needed a new coat of plaster. I felt pity for the two couples out there at the marketplace who were discussing how to tell me that my mother and grandmother had been deported to a concentration camp in the east . . .

I plugged in the vacuum cleaner, a noisy old thing that did not pick up much dirt any more, and started to vacuum the floor ferociously. Picking up the song where I had left off, I raised my voice over the thundering machine. I kept singing louder and louder, until I was shouting at the top of my lungs.

I stopped in front of the mirror and saw myself singing, my mouth open wide. The tears were making big wet splotches on my apron. I was singing as loud as I could so that I would not hear myself cry.

I picked up a face-cloth, rubbed my face, and went downstairs to wait for the others to come home.

20

Father

After Mother left on transport, we did not hear from her again. Father's health took a dramatic turn for the worse. His doctors would no longer let him get out of bed, and every letter he wrote to me sounded as if he expected it to be his last.

Utrecht, 31 May 1943
My only friend,
    I feel a great need to direct a few loving words to you, and to beg you not to be crushed by today's troubles. I myself am trying to resist it too, and I am prepared to face the days that remain to me with resignation. Sorrow I cannot feel any more, because those reservoirs are full to overflowing.
    Last week my brother Herman called. They have to 'evacuate'.* My sister Marie and her family too.† There is so much despair everywhere. That's why there is nothing for it but to wait and see what happens. Everyone has troubles. You too? Did Ineke fail her exams again? I am sorry if she did, even though it's not very important now. It's a failure of nerves – the girl can't help it.

---

  * By 'evacuate' Father meant that they had been ordered to report for transportation to Westerbork. Uncle Herman and his wife went underground at this point, having found a hiding-place in the home of a very religious Reformed Protestant family.
  † Aunt Marie and Uncle Louis and my cousin Annie were deported to concentration camps and never returned.

You'll note from this pencilled scribble that I am in bed. The doctor prescribed it. That makes writing tiring. But you need some news from me. My illness is somewhat stabilized. Fortunately, the doctors can help me with the pain. Without pain, everything else is easier to tolerate. Looking around, one sees not a single person free of trouble. It's just a matter of degree. And if you are young and of sound mind and healthy body, child, then you *must* use the sap of life to pull yourself through this temporary time of doom. You know that it cannot last for ever, and eventually everybody will be reunited, one perhaps a little more battered than the next; but that is because it has been a long war.

Oh, we – Hilde and I – have had our setbacks, and we still have them. Yet – even if we don't get through this, then what? We have had our lives, after all, we have founded a family. Set against our great happiness, we really can't complain now that a little unhappiness has come into our lives. We have enjoyed a full life, especially I. Many people never reach the age of sixty, some not even fifty. That is a consolation. For you children it has been a blessing to have enjoyed your parents' care for so long.

I have secured my *own* children's future as well as I could. All in good time, Uncle Lex and Tante Dop's husband will inform them and direct them as to the particulars.

As for you – don't let life ever get the better of you, do you hear? You have loving parents and so many friends that you need not be afraid of the future. Send your dear parents my heartfelt greetings. They have done more for us than any friend can be expected to do.

Goodbye, dear friend. You have brought me nothing but joy.

Your best old friend,
Doddel

Father filled his letters with ruminations about our happy past and told me not to give in to hate or despair. His letters now ended with messages like, 'Goodbye my angel – I will love you from beyond the grave.' I tried to close my mind to what he was saying. I was not ready to accept that the last remaining member of my family was about to leave me as well.

We had all been tiptoeing around the house while Ineke studied for her finals. This time, to everybody's great relief, she passed. Mrs z.K. decided it was time for her to pay Father another visit. She had heard that he was not doing well. I begged and pleaded to be allowed to accompany her, but she was firm. It was too dangerous now. The *Moffen* were hungry for more victims. They were stopping people on the street everywhere to check ID cards. I made Mrs z.K. promise that she would mention to Father how much I wanted to make the trip to Utrecht. If Father gave his permission, then she would have to let me go.

Utrecht, 17 June 1943
Dammit! I will not let myself go. Although it is a big effort to receive a visitor, I had the barber give me a complete beauty treatment so that when your foster mother gets back, she won't even recognize me. A haircut and a shave! Now I am sitting up in bed to write a few words to you – to show her that her visit has not been in vain. Indeed, I am tremendously happy that she has come to see me. When she arrived, they had just given me a morphine shot, so that at first I had some trouble recognizing her. She looked beautiful to me, wonderfully cool and reassuring. I am now struggling to finish reading your letter. The reason it is taking me so long is that my miss is such a Busy-Lizzie chatterbox – you do go on and on!

Oh, I sleep so much now, and I'm not always quite there

mentally. Also I hate it when I make mistakes when I write. Old age has its handicaps.

Well, as long as you young people are doing well. So – Ineke is doing better now, is that right? And it's just her father who was a little nervous? That too will pass. Besides, in fifty years we'll all be gone and it will be the turn of you young ones to carp and complain. (Funny how I keep misspelling everything.)

My love, my angel, everything within me is yours. Talking is almost impossible for me now, and that makes life difficult. Yes, we must hope for better times, do you hear? This week Mr Jansen visited me, together with the Houtzagers, his friends.* That was nice of them, wasn't it? I embrace you. No other news to tell. Stay faithful to me, my love!

Your most faithful, your friend,

Doddel

PS. Dearest, I'd rather you didn't come and visit me. Leave well enough alone. I haven't grown more handsome since you last saw me, and it's better that you remember me as I was.

All I could think of was that I wanted to comfort Father, who sounded so weak, so hopeless, and so *old*. I was crushed that he did not want me to visit him. I was sure that if only I could go to him, kiss his poor face and hold his hand, his health would immediately take a turn for the better. Surely he would recognize that I could take Mother's place and fill the great hole her leaving had left in him. I paced up and down my attic bedroom, fuming at the injustice of being cooped up here when there was so much to be done 'out there'. Mother, Jules, Omi – I had sat here helplessly while

---

* Mr Jansen was the next-door neighbour to whom Father had entrusted the sculpted bust; the Houtzagers lived down the street.

they were caught like fish in a net. Surely there was *something* I could do now!

Years later, when my own children were grown up, I came to the realization that I had been harbouring a feeling of resentment towards my father. I thought I felt that way because my father had rejected me by not letting me visit him in those last days of his life. It wasn't until 1988, when Miep sent me the following letter – which she had discovered in a box of forgotten papers in her attic – that I was to come to terms with the truth: I *had* been there. Not in person, but in a letter. In the end it was I who had given Father permission to let go of life.

Breda, 22 June 1943
Dear Father,

Here I am again, Papa – your comrade, your youngest pal, your child! This morning I got a letter from Aunt Dop in which she told me how you are doing right now. Doddeltje, I have been praying to God to take your pain away and end your suffering. You are so brave and so strong; I admire you so, especially your calm resignation.

Doddeltje – do you feel that I am near you? Do you feel that I am holding you in my arms now just the way you used to hold me when, as a little girl, something hurt or I couldn't sleep, or I was sad and needed your comfort? Now I am with you, your own, your only available loved one, and your hands are in mine. How good it must be to be released from your suffering and to be allowed to go to that world that knows no hate, no pain, no sorrow ... Doddeltje, you have been hoping for that moment to come soon, and you know, I wish that I could come with you, that I could follow you so that you will not be alone ... ! It will be so beautiful there, Father dear, with light –

bright colours – flowers – happiness and peace. Outside my window the birds are welcoming the arrival of summer, and I think that is the kind of music you will hear when your suffering is over.

Don't be sad, Doddeltje! If ever you do have to leave me, think of me with a light heart. You have given me so much support, such a world of love and so much beauty, and you have provided me (and the boys) with such a happy childhood – the very best foundation on which to build our lives. As for all the ugly things that have been happening, it is fate, it has nothing to do with us – it had to be so. And maybe it's best this way – if we had escaped, chances are some even greater tragedy would have been hanging over our heads. You and Hilde did everything, everything you could to save us and it worked, didn't it? Budi will return, I'm certain of it, and we'll make sure that he finds happiness again. Mother will return as well, and, Father – give me your hand – I give you my word by all that's holy, I hope this can reassure you – that *I'll* be there for them, I'll do what you expect of me: I *will* and *shall* be the pillar they can lean on. Father dear, you can count on me – I'll be strong – I'll take care of your loved ones – just rely on me, your youngest. If I were a royal princess, I would be considered an adult already. I am not afraid any more, and I promise that I'll be careful and protect my parents here [the z.K.s] in every way. I'll get through life; Guus and I will help each other later to complete the task you have set for us.

I hope I have not tired you too much. Today is Ineke's birthday. On behalf of all of us, especially you and Mam, I gave her a vase made of black tiles, and filled it with orange and yellow marigolds, Mam's favourite combination. Daddy, I have my arms around you now. Gently I kiss your forehead, your eyes, your cheeks, your hands . . .

I promise to accomplish the task you have given me. I'll keep my promises and I'll cope with life. Don't worry about me, nor about anyone else. Promise! You have given us all so much. We have supported one another; we have done all we could, and you have fought so bravely. Please don't brood any more. Let all your worries slip away, and just feel our love. Goodbye Daddy, dear Daddy. I kiss you once more, and I'll always be with you, from you and for you,
    Your child

I had entrusted this letter to Mrs z.K., who took the train to The Hague to hand it over to the Fernandes family. I enclosed a note to Aunt Jetty begging her to let Miep take the letter to Father at once and read it to him if he wasn't able to read it himself. Miep immediately took it to the hospital in Utrecht where, sitting at his bedside, she read it out loud to him.

This time, when the messengers arrived in Breda, I knew why they had come. I saw Aunt Dop's expression as she walked in, her arms stretched out to comfort me. Wordlessly, I fell into her arms. Father had died on 23 June 1943, just hours after receiving my letter.*

After I had been left to grieve for some time in my room – I don't remember how long, it could have been minutes or hours, sprawled on my bed, tense and aching – there was a soft knock on the door. Mrs z.K. and Aunt Dop, with tears in their eyes, encouraged me to come downstairs. It was time to discuss how we were going to handle this in public. The time had come to do the proper thing.

The neighbours and the family's relatives and friends knew

---

* Not long before her own death, Tine zur Kleinsmiede told my daughters what she had never been able to tell me – that she believed my father died by his own hand.

how very sick Nettie's father had been. Whenever they saw one of us, they always enquired after his health. They were always curious about me. After all, my stay had been lengthened from one summer to a full year by now, and, whether out of genuine sympathy or morbid interest, they couldn't help shaking their heads over the poor girl whose parents were unable to take care of her. In order to reaffirm my story, the z.K.s and the Verhulsts decided that the best thing to do would be to let it be known that Nettie's father had died in Utrecht.

When they heard about Father's death, the good people who knew me naturally wished to come by and offer me their condolences. But when they rang the doorbell, the z.K.s told them that Nettie had gone to Utrecht to bury her father, and would be away for three days.

For the next three days I was exiled to my room, being careful to stay away from the window. Ineke brought me food, and sometimes came and sat with me. After curfew, when the curtains were tightly shut for the blackout, I was allowed to come downstairs to spend a couple of hours with the family.

I had managed to obtain a cheap little lined notebook, and, unable to stop the habit of writing to my parents, I secretly continued to pour my heart out to them in it. It was not a diary – I dared not disobey Father's warning against writing a diary. But writing letters had always been permitted, hadn't it? Even if my parents were no longer around, what was the harm in continuing to write to them? So, alone in my room, I wrote and wrote, and, while writing, I cried. It was the only way I could let myself grieve.

Father dear, I don't know when it will finally register what it means, to have lost you – but I did promise you I would be brave, and so I will be . . . During the day I sometimes feel as if there is nothing wrong, and then it seems as if it isn't me this is happening to, but someone else; or that it's just a game, like any game; but then, when I am alone again, and I see you before me, and Mother, then I feel my heart . . . as if it's all broken in pieces, and the shards are sticking into my lungs and my throat . . .

Three days later, when Nettie 'returned from Utrecht', the visitors came to pay their respects and offer their condolences. For the first time since I had arrived in Breda, I was the centre of attention. I was no longer 'that girl from up north', or 'Ineke's little friend'. At last I had an identity: the poor girl who had just returned from her father's funeral and whose mother was still in hospital with complications from a broken hip. The visitors embraced me with tears in their eyes, and I responded obligingly with tears of my own. I was playing my part to perfection. Almost triumphantly, I sensed that I was reinforcing their belief that I was who I was supposed to be. Whatever doubts might have lingered in anyone's mind about me were finally put to rest. What a performance!

It was only after all the visitors had left that I realized that I had not just been playing the role of Nettie. I had also been playing Edith. Edith deserved their sympathy even more than Nettie, because she truly had lost everything. But that was something the visitors would never know.

21

Father's Shoes

It was Adrie who brought them. A pair of shoes, and the suit Father had worn while he was still strong enough to walk around the hospital grounds with his sketchbook.

I hung the charcoal grey jacket on a metal hook behind my attic door; the slacks were folded over a separate hanger. My hands patted the collar, lapel and sleeves. My cheek brushed the wide shoulders and rested against the padding, which formed a consoling cushion. I breathed in the familiar smell of Camel tobacco mixed with aftershave.

I inhaled deeply and closed my eyes, leaning against Father's jacket – an empty shell, its occupant gone for ever. Nothing left but a sweet scent, calling to mind a little girl sitting on Father's lap while he read from *Tom Sawyer*. His little girl – me.

Little? I had just turned eighteen, and I felt very old. On my birthday I had scribbled a 'letter' to Father in my secret notebook:

3 July 1943
Today I turned eighteen – the birthday that I looked forward to so much when I was younger, and so did you and Mother, the day when your youngest one would be all grown up – it has turned out quite differently from what I had expected. Now I am eighteen and I don't have a father any more – at least not a tangible one. I feel your presence close to me, but I can't see your dear face, or hear your soft, tender voice,

your jokes, your witty comments, your wise words, your songs, your enthusiasm for sports, your love – those I will have to miss for ever . . .

This morning was a morning like any other – quite different from the other years: no musical procession down the stairs to the gaily decorated birthday table, no suppressed impatience and excitement before being allowed to dig into the delicious birthday cake, no Mother, no Father, no wonderful happy day that always ended with my falling into your arms, exhausted, thanking you both from the bottom of my heart . . . Today I did not get a witty poem from you, no amusing drawing, no moving speech . . . but still I feel you are here . . .

I looked around to see where I had left the shoes. They were on the table in front of the window, on top of two piles of books. A pair of big old, black, wrinkled shoes, their noses pointing in the air. I sat down in my chair and stared at them. The inner soles were frayed and turned up at the edges; their colour, once tan, had darkened so that it too was nearly black. The weight of Father's body had made an imprint in the leather, leaving five dark circles where the toes pressed down on the sole. Three deep cracks made a diagonal mark from the top of each shoe where the big toe had lain buried to the opposite heel, crisscrossing like greyish veins all over the black leather. The soles, of a thick wartime substitute material, were unevenly worn, the heels sloping towards the outside.

After giving me Father's few belongings, Adrie had tactfully withdrawn, leaving me alone. He went to bed early that night, like the rest of the family. No one expected me to be sociable. I had little to say – to Adrie or anyone else. I felt empty of words.

It was to be Adrie's last visit to Breda. Everyone agreed it was no longer safe for him to make the trip. But our relationship was over in any case: it was time I admitted it to myself. For us, absence had not made the heart grow fonder. Since my move to Breda, there had been no kissing, no hand holding, no fondling during Adrie's infrequent visits. We had to keep our distance: here we were being held to Mrs z.K.'s strict standards of behaviour. In the absence of physical closeness, our love had inevitably cooled, and I had begun to assess our relationship with clearer eyes. For some time, I had been feeling that we were communicating on different levels. In my letters to Adrie, I had poured my heart out, showering him with philosophical questions about the meaning of life, confiding to him my deepest feelings and thoughts. I now saw that his responses had always been too shallow or superficial to satisfy my needs. Mother was right: in my isolation, in my impossibly vulnerable situation, I had come to rely too much on him. I had been making more of our relationship than it deserved. Being 'strong', I decided, also meant being self-sufficient. There was no room in my life now for schoolgirl romances. Adrie and I were to remain good friends, and nothing more.

I kept Father's shoes and his suit in my room for five months. But I knew I could not do so for ever. They had value – black-market value. Leather shoes had long been unavailable, and coupons for shoes of any kind were a thing of the past. Many people, not only farmers, had taken to wearing traditional Dutch wooden *klompen*, which are useful in sand or mud, but not very comfortable on the pavement or for wearing indoors.

I knew what was expected of me. I was to ride into the countryside, cycling from farm to farm to see if I could find anyone willing to trade the shoes for food.

Finally I summoned the strength to wrap the shoes in some old newspaper and tuck them into the basket hanging from the front of my bicycle with its tread-worn tyres. Without saying a word to anyone, I pushed the bicycle out of the shed and set off on my bartering expedition.

It didn't take long to find a customer. The third door on which I knocked was opened by a farmer's wife with whom my foster parents had done business in the past, trading a chicken for some fine linen sheets, towels, or other useful items. I cradled the package in my arms. 'I have some shoes here,' I began, hesitantly.

'Let's see them then,' she ordered.

Reluctantly I handed over the parcel and watched as she removed Father's shoes from the newspaper and turned them over and over in her hands, as if trying to gauge their weight, or estimate their size. I held my breath. I felt like a traitor.

I was on the point of telling her to forget it and grab the shoes out of her stubby red hands when she looked up and said, 'They are old and worn. They aren't worth anything much. But my husband could wear them to church. Or they may fit one of my sons. What do you want for them?'

It was not long before St Nicolaas, and I had wanted to present the z.K.s with a home-made gift, something good to eat perhaps, but I had no coupons for ingredients. 'Do you have any eggs, flour, or butter?' I asked.

The farmer's wife went into the house, and returned after a few minutes with a package wrapped in the same paper in which I had brought the shoes. Only the shape of the parcel was different now. 'Here, hide this under your coat. It's some cornmeal, a couple of eggs and a little bit of butter. That's all I can give you.'

It was enough to bake a cake.

The days oozed slowly by, like tar. Weeks became months, and a new year announced itself: 1944. We did not celebrate. After nearly four long years of war, we were too busy surviving the unrelieved dullness of every day. We fought for the crumbs left on the breadboard after Mrs z.K. had cut our rationed slices. Ineke and I would stand there until she was done, and then run our fingers over the splintery wood in search of crumbs, rolling them into little balls and popping them hastily into our mouths. We were now entitled to one egg a month per person, and the decision how to prepare the monthly treat was an agonizing one. Did I prefer mine boiled or fried? Or should we pool our eggs for pancakes, an omelette or mayonnaise? We could not make up our minds. Our mouths watered as we considered all the options. The anticipation was so exquisite that I was often let down by the reality when the 'day of the egg' finally came.

Allied forces had been advancing in Italy, and we tracked their progress with coloured pins on a map of Europe in Mr z.K.'s study. Mussolini was overthrown. The Soviets recaptured Ukraine and Crimea. The Germans were reportedly suffering great losses; yet even that news did not make any significant difference to the monotony of my days.

It had been a year and a half since anyone had called me Edith. The need to be convincing as Nettie was reinforced each time a new decree was published making it easier to catch Jewish fugitives. By now mass round-ups had virtually ceased: the country had been quite thoroughly emptied of Jews, except for the few (no one could guess how many) who had found a good hiding-place.*

I tried to incorporate Nettie Schierboom into my very self, and to bring her to life in my mind. I knew nothing about her, really, except that she was a housekeeper. I upgraded her status to 'mother's helper': I did not want to be the maid. As mother's helper, I could be a member of the family. I tried to picture Nettie, a girl from Wassenaar who had not had the

---

* The number of hidden Jews in Holland is now estimated to have been around 24,000. Of these, 8,000 were betrayed; 16,000 survived.

privileged upbringing that I had enjoyed, who was the same age as me but had gone into service at an early age. What was her life like? Did she know there was someone else walking around with her papers, masquerading as Nettie? If she knew, would she mind?

The thought of turning myself in still came up in my mind occasionally. I could just march over to Gestapo headquarters and tell them who I really was. 'Edith van Hessen,' I'd announce. 'Jewess.' Then I would be sent to Westerbork; at least there I would be with my own people, perhaps I would even meet up with friends or members of my own family. Yes, I'd have to work hard, but even a work camp seemed better than this terrible isolation and loneliness. I would have a chance of finding out if Mother or Jules were still alive. I would accept the destiny of my race. I never dared share these thoughts with the zur Kleinsmiedes, though.

One of our most reliable sources of forbidden news was 'To' (short for Antonia), the outspoken wife of a vegetable farmer who came to our house twice a week with a pushcart loaded with cabbages, potatoes and spinach. Sometimes she would even bring Mrs z.K. a poacher's rabbit hidden under a blanket. When To, who seemed permanently pregnant, stood at our front door discussing the political situation with my foster mother, grandly prophesying the war would be over by Easter, we all felt relieved and hopeful, and we believed her. But when we heard that Churchill had warned his own people and his allies that there were still months, years, of sacrifice and hard struggle ahead, we all shrugged our shoulders and agreed with To that Churchill was a miserable old pessimist and did not know what he was talking about.

Apart from potatoes and vegetables, To also grew strawberries on her farm on the outskirts of town. Strawberries were unavailable in the shops, since that crop, like much of the rest of the food produced in Holland, was earmarked for

German consumption. The intrepid To, however, was not inclined to let the Germans have their way, and she encouraged us to come and pick as many strawberries as we wanted before they were harvested.

One day in the late spring I was sent to To's farm to pick strawberries. The sun was warm and a strong wind was blowing at my back. I passed the barracks across the street, studiedly ignoring the German soldiers standing guard at the entrance, turned a corner and headed for the open road. My bike hobbled roughly over the cobblestones until the pavement turned to dirt and the terraced brick houses gave way to wheat fields. The wind in my back gave me a sense of freedom, and suddenly I felt excited to be alive. I began to hum, and then to sing.

First forcefully kicking the pedal down with my left foot, I'd coast for a few seconds, and then my right foot would come down, giving my bike another good spurt forward. Heady with the speed of my bicycle, the wide openness of the horizon, the wind tangling my hair, I found myself matching forbidden words to the rhythm of my pedalling. 'E-d-i-t-h!' I whispered to myself as my left foot came down, and then 'v-a-n H-e-s-s-e-n!' as I kicked the right pedal. Suddenly I was saying my name out loud, over and over again – '*Edith . . . van Hessen! Edith . . . van Hessen!*' The wonderful sounds, that I had missed for so long, rolled off my tongue effortlessly. 'EDITH VAN HESSEN!' I shouted exuberantly into the wind. 'EDITH VAN HESSEN!'

Suddenly the swaying wheat fields caught my attention. The stalks were waving in the wind, like an unruly sea. What was it they reminded me of?

Appalled, I clamped my lips shut. King Midas has ass's ears!

I suddenly remembered the legend of King Midas's barber who, having sworn never to tell anyone that under his master's great turban lurked a fair of donkey's ears, unburdened his secret by whispering it into a hole in the ground, which conveyed it to the reeds, which spread it to the wind, which carried the forbidden words to the four corners of the kingdom.

I got off my bike, and looked around anxiously. Was there anyone within earshot who could have heard me? What had possessed me? What if the wheat had the power to repeat my name, like an echo, and whisper it into some Nazi's ear?

Silently I got back on my bike and headed for To's farm. There I got on my knees and crawled between the rows of strawberry beds, digging my hands into the sandy dirt where the fruit lay half buried. The sun was warm, the berries ripe and juicy. All alone in To's garden, far away from the barracks, I crammed my mouth full of strawberries, savouring their sweet taste . . . and the memory of being Edith.

22

Crazy Tuesday

It was finally happening! The Allies were coming closer! The map in Mr z.K.'s study was slowly turning into a riot of colour as more and more orange, red, white and blue thumbtacks were stuck into formerly occupied territories with a satisfying twist of Mr z.K.'s wrist. The Allied forces had landed in Normandy, and were pressing on, with great losses, through France towards Belgium. I could not help worrying about my brother Guus. Was he among the Yanks who had landed on D-Day? Paris was liberated. But as the prospect of my liberation loomed nearer, so did my dread of what I might find out once the Germans were gone. As long as my parents had been around to do all the worrying, I had remained the eternal optimist, refusing to see life through anything but rose-tinted glasses. Now I had a new responsibility: to acknowledge the worst.

30 August 1944
To be honest, Father dear, I am comforted – happy, even – that you are no longer of this wretched earth. Even if you had recovered, even if you had been reunited with your loved ones, all this – this great injustice that can never be righted, the wrong that has been done to us, to our people, to some more than to others – it would all have been so impossible to forget, to go on with one's life as if nothing had happened. But Pappie, tonight I can't stop thinking

about our loved ones, out there in the unknown. Only you know, Pappie, whether they are still alive, whether they'll come back to me some day – I wish I knew. I am preparing myself never to see them again . . . then it can only turn out better than I expected . . . But the thought that while I am lying here in my cosy bed, they may be being tormented, humiliated, worked to death, or exposed to the cold or suffering or disease . . . Oh God, oh Father dear, please help them – save them!

Bands of dishevelled German soldiers were shuffling through Breda on their way home to Germany. It was the beginning of September 1944 and Brussels was under attack. We imagined that we could hear the thunder of the guns in the distance. We listened intently, trying to make out the sound of liberation.

Then, the dizzying news, spread by rumour, which contradicted the official reports of unshakeable German strength. Brussels had been liberated. Antwerp had fallen to the Allies the next day. Breda *had* to be next!

On 5 September, the day that was later referred to as '*Dolle Dinsdag*' (Crazy Tuesday), the entire country was in uproar. We were sure the end had come. In Breda, what had been a trickle of retreating Germans suddenly turned into a flood. There they came, the Germans, looking beaten and discouraged, in army trucks, civilian cars and even farm tractors. Some were on bicycles, some came on foot, pushing prams loaded with barrels and boxes. Stolen booty, we knew. There were civilians, too – turncoat Belgians who had collaborated with the Germans, and were now afraid to face the music at home. There were rumours that a good number of Breda's NSB-traitors were packing up their bags too.

Strengthened by the discouraged air of this rag-tag army, we were sure that this was the moment we had been waiting for so long. We came out of our houses and positioned ourselves boldly in the street, staring at the Germans, giving them ugly looks of silent accusation.

Suddenly one of our neighbours came running down the street. Breathlessly, he announced that the fleeing army had left at least a ton of butter behind. It was just lying there for the taking – in the heart of town, outside the Military Academy.

I did not hesitate a moment. I knew what I had to do. It was my duty to run as fast as I could to the Military Academy. This was an opportunity I could not pass up. I was going to grab what was due to us.

It was raining. There I was in a crowd of strangers, all of us running and splashing through the puddles like a bunch of excited children. The frenzied carnival atmosphere was catching. 'They' had taken everything from us. The thieves. Now it was our turn. If everybody else could be greedy, then so could I.

As I approached the Academy, I saw several open lorries being unloaded by men in overalls. Large cardboard barrels were being rolled down wooden loading planks. There was my butter! Pushing some people aside, I grabbed one of the barrels. Mine! I hung on to it for dear life, grinning wildly. Finally I was going to bring something useful home – a gift for the z.K.s. And what a gift! We had not seen butter in years. Even margarine was now a rare commodity.

There was no way I could carry the barrel. It was too heavy and unwieldy. I had to roll it all the way home, crossing the central marketplace, skirting the Singel Canal, passing through streets I had never visited in all my time in Breda. Finally, my hands blistered and my shins and knees covered with scratches, I reached Cavalry Street with my loot, breathless and triumphant.

In the kitchen Mr z.K. told us all to stand back. With hammer, pliers and screwdriver he started to work on the barrel. Ineke and I danced around him, getting in the way, trying to lend a hand.

Finally, the cover popped open. 'Careful!' we screamed, for the barrel was on its side, and something was spilling out of it. Out flowed a wave of coarse white powder with a strong disinfectant smell.

It was not butter I had captured. The barrel was filled with Vim – a common household scouring powder. This happened to be one of the few products that could still be bought in the shops without coupons. There was no soap to do the laundry, or to wash ourselves. But the sinks and toilet bowls were always sparkling clean. Vim was the one thing we had never been short of.

It was not the only disappointment that day. It turned out that the troops we had seen streaming through our town had been just the vanguard of defeat – a rout raised by rumour and discouragement. The Allies' advance northwards had been halted outside Antwerp. It was to be almost two more months until the liberators were truly at our doorstep.

I had to postpone my dreams of baking butter cakes and biscuits and threw myself into the task of doing something really useful: scrubbing the kitchen floor and the steps outside spotlessly, dazzlingly, clean – with Vim!

23

Liberation

When liberation finally came, on 29 October 1944, it still did not turn out quite the way we had expected.

For weeks we had lived in fearsome expectation. Explosions, fires, shooting, sniper fire – the fighting was now definitely within earshot. With no reliable information, we depended on guesswork. Rumour had it that the city of Maastricht, at the south-eastern tip of Holland, had been freed. We were beginning to see refugees from the countryside, people driven from their homes by the fighting. Nobody knew where the next assault would be coming from. By the end of October, nobody dared to go outside any more. People huddled inside their homes. For three long days we hid in the cellar, cringing every time we heard an explosion or the roar of guns.

Finally, Mr z.K. could stand it no longer. It was late afternoon on 29 October 1944, and things seemed to have quietened down somewhat outside. We argued about whether the sound of gunfire had turned significantly more sporadic and reluctant. With a cheerful, 'Well, I've had enough of this. The rest of you stay here – I'm going to see what's going on up there,' Mr z.K. stretched his limbs and cautiously ventured upstairs.

I hid my head between my knees as I listened for his footsteps upstairs. He was pacing heavily up and down, looking out of the front windows and the back. Finally he came back downstairs. 'There are Allied soldiers out there!' he announced with a big grin. 'They are crawling across the pavements. You can see them right in front of the house! You can come up now, I think. Come and see!'

As we peered out from behind the heavy curtains, a startling sight met our eyes. Bits of bushes and branches covered in autumn leaves seemed to be moving slowly along the low brick wall separating the front garden from the pavement, as if animated by invisible puppet strings. Suddenly we glimpsed green steel under the leaves – a helmet! Then more military helmets, all camouflaged with leaves and branches. Soldiers crouching in battledress. Young. Delightful. Grinning. Allied soldiers! At one end of the street we could see armed Germans running away, out of the barracks, while at the other end Allied tanks were approaching. It was chaos. The sound of gunfire was all around us. We were right in the middle of a battle!

We stayed away from the windows and dived on to the floor when a particularly heavy barrage was heard. Finally an eerie silence descended. Not a sound. Two minutes passed. Then five. Stillness. Once again, Mr z.K.'s inquisitiveness got the better of him. Cautiously he opened the door and walked out to the gate. We could see him standing there, his hands in his pockets, assuming the same stance with which he used to welcome Herr Niemke home from the barracks at night. This time, however, his frown disappeared and a warm smile spread over his face. A soldier in khaki was approaching. Mr z.K. and the soldier shook hands, and then Mr z.K. slapped the soldier heartily on the back.

The soldiers who liberated us were members of the First Polish Tank Division.* The entire neighbourhood was out in the street now, dancing, jumping up and down, and hugging

* Of the Free Polish Army, composed of soldiers who had escaped the German occupation.

each other. Nobody could quite believe that it had really happened. The Poles and the Canadians and the British were here! The Germans were driven out! More and more Allied soldiers in their jeeps and tanks came pouring triumphantly into our street. We waved at them, pumped their hands, and kissed them. I will never forget what became for me the smell of liberation: the aroma of leather mixed with cigarette smoke and gasoline.

Suddenly Mrs z.K. grabbed my hand and pulled me over to a group of dazed, happy revellers. 'Friends!' she announced triumphantly. 'I have something to tell you!'

I felt all eyes on me, and started to blush.

'You always thought this was Nettie Schierboom, didn't you?' said Mrs z.K. 'Well, she isn't. Her name is Edith van Hessen.' She put her arm around my shoulder, and went on proudly, 'Let me introduce her to you. This girl of mine. This is Edith.'

I was embarrassed, but also proud to be a part of Mrs z.K.'s big moment. I danced around, allowing people to hug and congratulate me. Some neighbours exclaimed they would never have guessed. Others nodded knowingly. One lady burst into tears and squeezed me in a bear hug as if I was her long-lost daughter.

'We did it!' beamed Mr z.K. 'We really did it!' Finally, we trooped back inside to taste the bottle of wine that Mr z.K. had saved for this day – a day, he assured us, he had always known would come.

Suddenly we heard shooting again. It was coming from very nearby. The Germans had launched a counter-attack! The Poles scampered into the tanks, and positioned themselves behind their guns. More tanks moved into the street. A sniper who had managed to hang on to his position in the water tower behind our house had begun to shoot wildly in every direction.

Mr and Mrs z.K. looked at each other in alarm. Had they made a terrible mistake in letting our secret out too soon? What if the Allies were pushed back? Would anyone betray us? My foster father shouted at us to get down on the floor. For what seemed like an eternity, we lay on the dining-room floor, berating ourselves for not keeping our mouths shut a little longer. Desperately I prayed to God, and begged him not to do this to us now that the end was in sight.

Finally, the shooting stopped. The sniper had been silenced. The Germans were well and truly gone. Sheepishly we all trailed outside again, to continue where we had left off.

During the years I had been living in Breda, we had always kept very much to ourselves. I had appreciated the zur Kleinsmiedes' strategy of avoiding suspicion by having as little to do with outsiders as was (politely) possible, and I had not found it hard to remain inconspicuous. No doubt some of the neighbours had had something to hide as well. Mr z.K. had taken part in Resistance activities, disseminating information – even Ineke and I had clandestinely stuffed neighbours' letter-boxes with anonymous leaflets after these had mysteriously made their way into our own. You never talked about it, however, because you never knew where you might run into a traitor. But now, suddenly, we felt close to our neighbours. We needed to reach out to each other, to break down the barriers of suspicion and celebrate as a group.

The celebration was somewhat tempered by the knowledge that so far only a small part of Holland was free. But surely that was only a matter of time! Soon, we were certain, the entire country would be rid for ever of the hateful occupiers.

The good people of Breda lost no time in rounding up the collaborators as well as the women ('Whores!' we yelled) who had 'befriended' German officers and soldiers. I watched with glee as the girls' hair was shaved off and thrown into the angry crowd while they were paraded through the streets in open lorries. I yelled at them as loudly as everyone else, shaking my fist, swept up by the pent-up anger and hatred all around me. It was a thrilling sensation to belong to the aggressors, and no longer to the victims.

The population was now divided into 'good' and 'bad': everything was black or white. There were heroes, and there were villains. The zur Kleinsmiedes definitely belonged to the heroes. I, too, was 'good', merely by virtue of my status as hidden Jew. (Later I often found myself wondering what I would have done had I had any choice. Would I have risked my life to save someone else's? That thought made me more tolerant of the people who had done nothing, and stayed out of trouble; who were neither good nor bad, and of whom there were plenty.)

It was a day that marked the end of fear – and the beginning of sorrow.

Now that I had 'surfaced', my position in the zur Kleinsmiede family changed. They went to even greater lengths than before to make me feel that I was one of them. I was grateful, but sometimes I felt a little awkward about this turn of affairs, since I spent every waking moment dreaming of being reunited with my *real* family.

One day, soon after liberation, I found a little blank note-book on my pillow, dedicated to me by Ineke with these words:

Sunday, 12 November 1944
Today is an important day. Why? Because today I am giving you this notebook, so you can turn it into a diary. It's nothing great, it's just a flimsy exercise-book, but it'll have to do for now, little sister. Yes Edith, you are truly a little sister to me now. Perhaps you don't have as much of a need of a sister as I do, because you have Guus and Jules

– and Miep and Nina were like sisters to you before I came along. Perhaps my sentimental rambling leaves you cold. That's all right too. But darling, every person must make a daily reckoning of his own conscience, which is a hard enough thing to do. May this little book help you in that endeavour.

Eagerly I took up where I had left off when I first went into hiding, and started scribbling in my journal – openly.

13 November 1944
A new diary, this time given to me by my sister. We were visited by a lot of Poles again this weekend. Mr Rolfsky played the piano, beautifully. Great guys. Tobias, Hilchner, Barges, Rolfsky, Pindensky – every evening another contingent shows up. It's so crazy that it's impossible to get any work done. Socks to be darned? Forget it! Had a haircut Saturday. There is so very little to be had with your ration card these days. Still, a wonderful atmosphere in town. When I got home I found I had just missed Frank Zaluscovsky, who is going to England in a few days. He is going to try to find out about Guus for me. And he promised to post a letter from me to Washington, to Mr Ritter (Guus's employer). Mrs z.K. went to the Red Cross for me today, to ask about Guus. I didn't get anywhere with them when I went.

Today Mr z.K. put a jar on the table, in which everybody has to deposit a one-cent fine every time they call me 'Nettie'. When the jar is full, we'll use the money to go out to dinner.

V-1s* are exploding over Brussels and Antwerp. The north of the province of Brabant is in terrible shape. Four

---

* Unmanned long-distance 'revenge' rockets launched by the Germans towards the end of the war.

thousand people from Zevenbergen have been evacuated to Breda, those people don't have anything, just the clothes on their backs. Ineke and I have signed up as volunteers in the KVV (Female Volunteer Corps).

The barracks across the street were now filled with Polish soldiers of the First Tank Division, and everyone opened their houses to them. We pasted signs in our windows saying '*Dziękujemy wam Polacy*', which meant 'Thank you, Poles!' My foster parents invited officers they met to have meals with us, and we communicated as best we could in a mixture of English, German and gibberish. The spare bedroom, that had remained largely unoccupied since Herr Niemke, was now graciously offered to any officer needing a place to stay. Having all these men around suddenly reminded me of my life in The Hague, where our house had always been full of my brothers and their friends. But I was also immediately aware of the difference. Here it would not do to be flirtatious. That sort of behaviour was frowned upon by my foster family. Besides, these soldiers were quite a bit older: they were the adults' friends, not mine and Ineke's. Almost all of them had wives at home.

It took me a little while to start savouring my new freedom. That I was free to go out, to go anywhere I liked, without fear, was a concept that took some getting used to. But gradually I began to understand that I was truly at liberty, so long as I got the z.K.s' permission (it took years for me to shake off the mantle of 'obedient' girl). I was eager to be of service, to do some good, to find out if any other Jews had made it through. I heard about a little Jewish boy suffering from a fatal illness who had been hidden in a Christian nursing home on the other side of town. One morning I set off to visit him, armed with some goodies and books.

To reach the clinic I had to cross a bridge that was guarded by a member of the Dutch Resistance Army. The man was checking everyone's ID papers; there were still traitors around, and it was the Resistance fighters' job to ferret them out.

I proudly handed the man my precious ID card, identifying me as the Gentile Nettie Schierboom from Wassenaar. It was the first time in all the years since I had gone into hiding that anyone had asked to see it.

The fighter scrutinized my card, turning it around and squinting at it in the sunlight. Then he turned back to me and looked from me to the picture, and back again. Finally he smiled. 'Whoever did this made an excellent job of it,' he said. 'Congratulations. But it's false, of course.'

Weakly I smiled back. I thought of my brother Jules, and how he would laugh when he heard the story. A sadness gripped me. I had a strong feeling of foreboding about Jules. That he might not come back from the east; that he might never have the chance to laugh at the Resistance fighter's back-handed compliment.

I also realized that my forged ID would never have stood up to an inspection by the Germans.

We were liberated – and yet I was not free. It was to take the Allies another six long and painful months to push through to the north of Holland. In the meantime it was useless to attempt to find out what had happened to Omi, Jules and Mother. A curtain had fallen between the occupied and liberated parts of the country: there were no avenues of communication open. No more visits from Adrie or his parents. No letters from Miep or any other friends. In a sense, I was more isolated than ever before.

15 November 1944
Nina's birthday. Back in September we had made plans to

celebrate it together. And now? Now we are liberated and happy, while in The Hague – who knows what they are going through right now. Nineke, I wish you all the best, and hope you'll make it through this horrible time. Tonight I'll drink a toast to you, and am thinking of you.

The fine for the Nettie jar has been raised to ten cents. I really do want to call Mr and Mrs z.K. 'Aunt' and 'Uncle', because I call Aunt Dop and Uncle Aa that, and they aren't even my foster parents. So from yesterday, I had to start contributing ten cents for every time I call them Mr or Mrs. Well, I was down one guilder in no time at all. So my fine has been cut in half, to five cents, since I am twice as likely to make a mistake as they are. The jar is pretty full already. I find it terribly hard to say Uncle Eb and Aunt Tine. Today Ineke and I unearthed some more of the hidden copper and silver from under the floorboards.

I wish that, some way or other, I could get hold of Guus. He has missed so much, how he must long to see one of us, especially if he has given up all hope on everyone. I also long for Paul, who I suspect might be in the Princess Irene Brigade,* which is stationed in Wuestwezel, but Uncle Eb says he had rather I didn't go, which I quite understand.

The Allies' advance ended at the major rivers to the north of Breda, where the enemy had dug in for a decisive fight. The pivotal Battle of Arnhem was waged so nearby that we thought we could hear the explosions from our house, and the constant rattle of anti-aircraft guns disturbed our nights. We were worried about the Koperbergs, who were trapped on the other side of the river, cut off from their sole lifeline, us, their friends in Breda.

It was a long and severe winter. Over the radio, we heard

---

* A division of Dutch exiles.

about unimaginable hunger and suffering in the North. The railways had gone on strike,* electricity had been cut off. People were ripping apart abandoned houses and even stripping their own homes for firewood. Nor did the beleaguered occupiers have any interest in keeping the urban population supplied with food. Everything grown in Holland was for the German troops, or sent on to Germany. In Amsterdam, people were eating tulip bulbs, sugar beets and cats! When we heard that, we stared in misery at our plates, where our meagre rationed meals suddenly seemed disgustingly rich and abundant. Ineke and I felt frustrated, helpless. If only there was something we could do to help!

> In the North it is a time of terror right now. No, this is not a time to be relieved or happy. Still, the chocolate Mr Tobias [a Polish officer who was briefly a house guest] brought me from Belgium tastes ridiculously delicious. It's been so long since I had some.

I dreamed of bumping into my brother Guus. Even though it had been years since I had heard from him, I was convinced that he had joined the US army, and hoped that he was among the liberators. But I knew that it was just as likely that he had either stayed behind in the US or been sent to the Pacific. I prayed that he was still alive. I asked every man in uniform I met if he knew a Guus van Hessen. Often, walking down the street behind a soldier in camouflage dress, I would convince myself that I recognized my brother's back. My heart pounding, I would run to overtake him, only to discover to my embarrassment that the man looked nothing like Guus.

Ineke was increasingly open about her affection for me, and that provided some measure of comfort, though it was no release from the feeling I had of being stifled and constrained,

---

* By order of the Dutch government-in-exile in London.

especially since she was in the habit of reading my diary and occasionally wrote messages to me in it. I had to be careful what I wrote.

17 November 1944

Last night I went to bed early. Ineke came and sat next to me. After tucking me in, she stayed sitting next to me in the dark for quite a while. Just like a little mother. She told me to go to sleep, but first we talked, in the dark. During the day there's too much going on – you think about the hallway floor you just cleaned, the piles of socks needing to be darned, the potatoes that are waiting to be peeled, and how dirty your fingernails are. Last night was, in contrast . . . intimate. Today we gave the kitchen and hall a thorough cleaning. This evening a visit from Tobias and Rolfsky, the pianist. Such a nice man. He had been married for just two days when he had to escape from Poland. When I think of what those men have been through . . . I hear those Poles talking about their narrow escapes from Nazi territory, and I find just a little crumb of hope – perhaps Jules too has managed to get away, some way or other? Who knows?

I met a Jewish family from Breda, the van Buerens, who had come out of hiding and reclaimed their own home. I witnessed the relief and joy of their reunion with family members and friends. I was happy for them, but seeing their happiness also increased my pain. I had expected to feel closer to those who had shared my predicament; being with them just made me feel more cut off.

1 December 1944

We went to the van Buerens', there was quite a gathering, all kinds of Jewish soldiers and people who had come out of hiding. Still, I was disappointed. As usual, my expectations had been too high – about the atmosphere, the mentality of the people who have come out of hiding. It's just that I can't stand all the griping these days. That terribly bitter Jewish soldier from Poland showed up again, who couldn't stop cursing the Poles and went on about the anti-Semitism over there again. Oh please – it makes me want to throw up.

Some nights earlier, at a social for the military, I had sat at a table with this 'terribly bitter' man and some other Jewish soldiers from the Polish Brigade. At the end of the evening, when the Polish, Canadian, British and Dutch national anthems were played, my Polish table partners had refused to stand for theirs. I did not know what to think – after all, the Poles were our liberators. How could these very Poles, who had risked their lives for our freedom, who were such charming guests when they came to visit the z.K.s – how could these same people tolerate anti-Semitism and, if my table companions were to be believed, make army life unbearable for their Jewish comrades-in-arms?

The other problem was that I felt I could not go anywhere without Ineke, and Ineke was simply not a very sociable girl. If I managed to persuade her to come with me to a celebration, her dour, shy and critical presence put a dampener on everything, and made me realize there really wasn't much joy in dancing and partying any more.

2 December 1944
I did enjoy the dancing a little last night, I couldn't help myself. As long as it is not one of those empty affairs where you find yourself cavorting with total strangers, where there's nobody you know. Besides, what's the use of partying and dancing now, when there is so much suffering and you don't have any news of anyone. In Utrecht – and all the other cities to the north of the big rivers – it's just

terrible. We heard that you have to pay thirty-five guilders for a kilo of potatoes; a guilder for a kilo of potato peel! I wonder how Flip Zwarts is? He must be in Germany by now, or wherever, because Westerbork has been emptied for the use of NSBers. Is he still alive, I wonder? And what about Miep, Nina and all the others in The Hague? I just cannot imagine what they are going through. Adrie must have gone into hiding – I bet he's with the Resistance.

It is strange, but I can't stand it any more when people ask me about my family. From now on I just won't tell them much. I will just say: 'Poland.' That's all. Because, of course, they feel sorry for me, and then they want to do something for me, something friendly, something cheering and consoling, but I don't want people to feel sorry for me, I feel the need to cheer up others, to give others courage, rather than to be the recipient of the same. I would so like to *do* something – for the Netherlands – for our people – for all the Dutch who have suffered. I want to roll up my sleeves and work, really work – and to show my foster parents that I am good for something. Because I *can* do it and I *want to* do it. But what?

I don't know anything about nursing. I can't go to England to be trained for the army, too young, and besides, here they would not let me go. Dammit, why isn't there anything that I can do? I have been passive for two and a half years, I just let everything come to me, even Ineke – just accepted everything, love, consolation, a home – but now, now surely the time has come for me to give something back? Now wait a minute, Edith, don't do anything too hasty, take your time, think everything through first.

Sometimes I'm so afraid that Guus is not alive. Still, I hope fervently that he is fighting for us, that he is helping all our men for the liberation of the Netherlands, of the East Indies, for the freedom of Mother, Jules, all our friends.

Most of the time you can stay cool inside, and calm – but then again you get such a terrible longing for home, the home you left behind, with Mother and Father and the boys. That you may never have that again – it's hard to accept. Strange, it hurts at the bottom of your skull, in the back of your throat – is that your heart that you feel aching? Silly girl.

A nearby Dutch concentration camp, Vught, was now in the liberated territory. The stories of inhuman cruelty that trickled out of there didn't leave much room for hope.

I have been reading a report of an ex-prisoner of the camp Vught, an eyewitness. It was awful, and it shows that I shouldn't have too much hope of ever seeing them again. And that was just Vught, here in Holland – what can it be like in Poland?

He writes that one day a group of SS men decided to have some fun at the expense of a Jewish prisoner. He had been assigned to work in the forest, digging trenches and chopping wood. The SS guards ordered the prisoner to jump into a trench to catch a frog. Sloshing around in the slimy mud, he managed to catch one. He was told to eat it, and if he didn't – bang bang. What else could the man do but swallow the animal alive? Then he was given another order: to fetch something from a trench some distance away. 'But I can't do that!' he said. 'I was told that leaving my group was punishable by death!' 'We don't give a damn,' his tormentors laughed. 'Run! Or we'll shoot you!' So he ran, and they shot him in the back anyway – 'for trying to escape'. Pregnant women were beaten on their bellies, were herded into trains with hardly any clothes on; the Jews, everything taken from them, headed into the Polish winter. How can God permit this sort of thing . . . ? Oh Mother dear, please come back!

Ineke and I were invited to parties and dances held to entertain the Allied soldiers. But, influenced by my uptight family (Aunt Tine warned us that kissing was 'filthy', and Ineke usually wanted to leave the dance as soon as we got there), I was unable to enjoy myself. I felt used, and was shocked and disgusted when a married officer seemed to expect a goodnight kiss (and more) from me after he escorted me home. Still, I realized that I was using the men too, since I asked any soldier who was likely to travel to London on leave to help me trace my brother. The British and Poles showered us with white bread (it tasted like cake!), chocolate and soap; they, in turn, appreciated the fact that both Ineke and I spoke English fluently.

I often went to the nursing home to visit the dying Jewish orphan Harry. I felt I had more in common with this twelve-year-old than with anyone else in Breda. I had given Harry my old accordion, and he was teaching himself to play it.

15 December 1944

Yesterday evening visited Harry. He was in great pain. Still he insisted on showing me he could play the Wilhelmus,* with one finger. The sisters were very impressed, he said. He was gasping for breath – someone had to hold the instrument for him.

He had a fever. He talked seriously about God. Wouldn't it be better if God put an end to this life – so lonely, so young, so damaged and so incurable? His wound is open, and full of pus. Last night you could just about hear it fester. You see him shrinking before you, and he looks at you with those big dark eyes. 'If it bothers you, just tell me,' he said. If he's angry or in a bad mood, who can blame him? He has the prospect of a long and endless night – the

---

* The national anthem, 'Wilhelmus of Nassau'.

sleepless night that's hard enough if you're healthy – all alone, without a mother that he can call out to and who'll come and hold his hand . . .

Last night I had to think about how I keep reassuring Ineke: 'What makes you think one of those V-1s is going to land here, of all places – on *our* house or on Breda?' But then what do *I* think about Jules and Guus? Am I not afraid they are dead? Don't I think, 'So many millions of young men have been killed or murdered, why should my brothers' lives be spared?' Paul, too. I reproach Ineke for not having faith . . . yet I'm just as scared as she is. Sometimes I'm so afraid . . .

19 December
Yesterday I was not allowed to see Harry – his fever was too high. Today he was a little better. I had to play a tune for him – but it isn't easy for me, I'm not in the mood, especially not in a hospital, surrounded by so much pain. Besides, before, with Mother, Jules, Father and all of us, it was fun to sing, but that's all gone, the song is just gone. Sunday night I missed Guus so terribly – because at the moment he is everything to me, father, mother, brother all rolled into one. Ineke did her best to comfort me in bed, with her arms wrapped around me. She played Chopin's lullaby, *Tristesse*, for me just now – it's so beautiful . . .

When I could get away from my domestic duties at home I did volunteer work, cooking and cleaning in a shelter for evacuees. Washing dishes in another kitchen with other girls was a welcome break in the monotony of my life. The harder I worked, the better I felt. There was a cold spell; the sight of skaters enjoying themselves just made me sad.

29 December 1944
People are skating on the ponds and lakes. It does not tempt

me at all, the way it used to. Without Jules and the rest –
no, I couldn't. It would bring back too many memories.

No news at all, despite all our enquiries – from any
quarter. Just two more days and then this wretched year
will be over.

31 *December*

New Year's Eve . . . This year we all have to 'celebrate' it
on our own . . . Mother, Guus, Jules . . . Omi? . . . and me.
I think of them all – of Miep, her parents, Nina, Adrie and
his parents, all our friends, all the good people in the (as
Radio Oranje just said so eloquently) bitter north. It's such
a horrible time. How is the rest of the world marking the
end of 1944? It's not a night to celebrate. There was a piece
in the paper about Buchenwald in 1938 – horrors. I feel
terribly empty. Perhaps next New Year's Eve will be different. With Mother and the boys? Don't count on it.

Still, now we are all sitting together downstairs – warm
wine and apple fritters – but not really in a celebratory
mood. That is for next year, when Holland will be completely free . . . 1945, you'd better make sure that everything
turns out all right up there – that they all survive the terrors
in one piece, that Holland is spared and not destroyed –
and then please won't you bring my mother and brothers
back? And the whole family. Nineteen forty-five – there's
so much for you to do – but you are young, you can do it!

This time, for the first time in four years, my New Year's
wish was to be partially granted.

One gloomy day in January, when Aunt Tine was trying to
console me as I sat sobbing at the kitchen table, the doorbell
rang. I jumped up, rubbing my face with my apron. 'I'll go,'
I announced. A visitor was always a welcome relief.

A tall officer in RAF uniform flashed a radiant smile at me. He lifted his cap. 'Eetje,' he said, simply.

'Paul!' I shrieked.

16 January

Paul and Guus have been found!!!! Sunday I was down in the dumps and Aunt had just said to me that morning, 'Who knows, maybe Guus will be standing at our doorstep this afternoon.' And what do you know, at three o'clock Paul was at our doorstep! He found my name in London on a list of people who'd come out of hiding. He came here via Maastricht. He was laden with stuff for us. Has not changed. Looks so much like Jules. He is a lieutenant in the RAF – a Mitchell plane pilot, he is dropping bombs on Germany. He's stationed at an airbase 10km outside Brussels. He has flown three missions out of fifty so far. He has been through a lot. But he's just the same old Paul. I couldn't believe my eyes. And Guus????? Guus is a sergeant in the US army. Paul has seen him and talked to him a couple of times. Guus was given leave twice so far to look for me – he was in Maastricht etc. I might really see him soon! He is at the front – at the place where the Jerries have been pushing their counter-offensive. He is a radio operator in the artillery. Boy, am I happy! The two days that Paul was here were wonderful. It's too good to be true, that both of them have come back to me. Now I can write to them.

In the spring of 1942, my cousin told me, he had crossed the border into Belgium with the help of a farmer who lived just a few miles from where we were now. In Lyon, the honorary consul of the Netherlands, who happened also to have been a colleague of Paul's in the family firm S. v. Hessen & Co., provided him with papers to cross into Spain and from there to the Dutch West Indies. After a few days in a

Spanish prison, he had been allowed to board a ship in Cadiz bound for Curaçao. His ship was part of a flotilla of fifty-five that came under heavy German attack. Only twenty-nine ships reached their destination. After joining the Dutch army in Curaçao, Paul was sent to Canada to be trained as a fighter pilot in the RAF, and now he was finally flying bombing missions over Germany – 'doing my bit to end this bloody war'.

Now that I had Guus's military field number, I wrote to him almost daily. But it was to take four months before I finally had a reply from my brother.

These last few months of the Second World War were perhaps the most difficult that I had yet experienced. I was constantly on the verge of tears. The years of hiding had taken their toll on me, and I was afraid that they had left me an empty shell, good for nothing except cleaning houses. Remaining optimistic was hard, even though I continued to cling to whatever crumbs of hope were to be found.

10 February 1945
Just heard over the radio that 300 Dutch people have arrived safe in Switzerland, inmates of a Jewish concentration camp in Theresienstadt . . . Mother?

22 February 1945
Why do you keep hoping, even when you know there's no hope left? I went to the van Buerens because they have the list of the freed Dutch Jews from Theresienstadt now in Switzerland. Mother's name wasn't there – nobody's. Except Phil Dwinger* and wife, and Renée's uncle Louis Kiek, and Aunt Map's brother. It's not that I had expected anything, really – but on the way home I almost collapsed. What an idiot.

* My physics teacher at the Jewish Lyceum.

I have such a need to cry these days – just for a few minutes, and then it's over, and I laugh at myself. When I ride past houses, I think to myself, 'What would it be like to live there?' and even if they are ugly houses, I know that if I lived there and I came home and Mother was waiting for me inside, how lovely it would be! At every house I picture how it would be, with Mother standing by the window arranging flowers . . .

My worst day was the day that we heard Paul's plane had been hit. Luckily he had been able to land safely, but he had been wounded in the shoulder. He was now in hospital in Brussels.

27 February 1945
I don't think I have ever felt as bad as I feel today. This morning had a crying fit in my room, Ineke sitting beside me. I feel so awful, so lost sometimes – I can't really explain what it is. Sometimes you feel like a totally isolated piece of human meat that someone is using as a spinning top. I feel I don't belong anywhere – everyone I know, I have known only since I went into hiding. Everything hurts me these days – I just don't know how to be fun like before. Either I'm dull and a drag, or I'm a maniac – busy, hateful and fussy. (So says Ineke.) And I'm so dissatisfied, so frustrated! I want to work, work towards a goal, do something for Holland, for the people who are returning, and not that boring house-cleaning, day in day out. But there's nothing else for it, I have to stay here, I'm needed here. And – this has nothing to do with Aunt and Uncle and Ineke, really – sometimes I *hate* Breda, I miss The Hague so much, I miss my friends, our house, the people I love – not all these new superficial acquaintances. Because everything here reminds me of two and a half years of Mother gone, Father gone, Jules gone, Omi gone – everything, everything gone. It's as

if it's suddenly more difficult for me now. What never used to bother me, bothers me now. This morning Aunt Tine told the chimney-sweep, 'Just ask the girl upstairs to show you her attic window.' The 'girl upstairs'? To be the girl, the maid, it never bothered me before, but now, now that I am Edith van Hessen again, and free – now I've lost all my self-confidence. I've forgotten everything that I used to know, everything that used to define me as Hilde van Hessen's daughter. Guus and Paul won't be proud of me this way. Soon, when Holland is liberated, people will ask me, 'And what did *you* do for our country?' and then I'll have to reply, proudly, 'I kept the house clean.'

24

Peace

When the USA was drawn into the war at the end of 1941, Guus had been called up into the army. Putting his boyhood hobby to good use, he became a radio operator with the 30th Army Division and landed in Normandy several days after D-Day. In September 1944, Guus was one of the few Dutchmen to take part in the liberation of Maastricht, the first Dutch city to be freed from the Nazi occupation. Upon contacting the Red Cross there to obtain information about his family, he was told that all of us – his parents, grandmother, brother and sister – had survived and were living safely somewhere in Holland. Jubilantly, he had telegraphed relatives and friends in England and America to tell them the good news. But the next day, he received word that it had all been a mistake. 'However,' the Red Cross told him consolingly, 'we are positive that your sister, at least, is alive, and is living in Breda.'

Guus was so shaken and discouraged by this turn of events – 'the coldest shower of my life', he said – that he did not believe this last piece of information provided by the Red Cross. He was in no mood to have his hopes dashed again, so he discontinued his search. Soon after his division was sent into the Battle of the Bulge, and my letters failed to reach him until several months later.

So there I was, waiting for some word from the sole other survivor of my family . . . with nowhere to go, and nothing to do but worry. Still, when spring came, I couldn't help being influenced by the optimism of the trees. They were covered in gorgeous blossom, and the air around me exploded with their fragrance.

26 March 1945
I often have this feeling inside that 'I want to be happy, I *will* be happy – I can take what life doles out, even if all it brings is bad luck.' You can take a lot. And life will turn out to be beautiful – if you can come up with something to give to others, instead of always taking.

It gives you courage, this feeling of strength, of being strong enough to take on life. It helps you survive a lot. I wish that I could give Ineke some of this courage, because in this we are so different. She doesn't think life is beautiful – and she believes that things will always go badly for her. Sometimes I can't blame her, because sometimes I have to admit that this life makes you feel as if you're choking to death. The war, the suffering, the hate – what is it all for? But now that spring is here and suddenly you see flowers in all the gardens, every day a new flower – then you realize that it is not all black, what life has to offer. Besides, wasn't my life, until this time, sunny, just as it was for Jules and all of us? Sometimes you think, how unfair life is. The van Buerens, who have their own home and their own things back, just like before, having people over, their children were on the list of survivors from Theresienstadt, their sister safe and living next door again, and then for another, everything gone . . . very little left, and then what is left, is unreachable . . . Because what that's all about, that silence from Guus, I can't imagine, since I've had a number of reports, via England, that people have seen him, but from him, nothing.

Finally, on 29 March 1945, a postcard from Guus. A letter followed.

1 April 1945
Darling,

As you see I will keep my promise and write to you as often as possible. You cannot imagine how much your 'big brother' longs to see you . . . We have so much to tell each other, everything that has happened over the past five years, how hard I worked to get you out of there, either to America or to Cuba, and all about the rest of my life in that enormous country. I just got a letter from Mr and Mrs Ritter today, expressing their condolences about Father. They are the finest and best friends that we had outside Holland, and I'll never be able to thank them enough.

Oh and, Ee, I have a girlfriend in America, which might interest you, as my sister, my mother and my I-don't-know-what-else. I'll show you her picture when I visit you.

Well, darling, just keep your chin up and rest assured that there is someone who is always thinking of you and whom you can consider not just as a brother but also as someone to take the place of your dear parents.

A sturdy handshake and much love, and my warmest greetings and wishes to 'Uncle', 'Aunt' and Ineke.

Your loving brother,
Guus

And then, an avalanche of letters, not only from Guus and Paul but also from friends from my old life who were beginning to reappear as more and more regions were set free. The Germans were being squarely beaten, and the war was almost over. Suddenly I was walking on air – and I had to deal with a foster sister who was sliding into depression. The happier I was, the more afraid Ineke became that she was losing me.

14 April 1945
A good day today. The sun was shining this afternoon as if it was summer. Behind To's farm, in the meadows,

there were buttercups and daisies and dandelions in full shimmering splendour – I was in seventh heaven. There is post again between Limburg and Brabant [the two southern provinces] and today I got a card from Guus and from . . . Dicky!!! Oh, how happy I am that he is OK. Rob too. Marcel was here and told us he visited the newly liberated areas of Holland.* I wish I could visit Germany too and gloat over how those bastards have been crushed. Arnhem – Assen – Coevorden – Westerbork are all set free; the Allies have reached Groningen! The Russians are getting ready to attack Berlin – Hanover has been taken – Celle liberated (the camp that had only 197 survivors) – the *Moffen* are finished!

Now that I have Guus again, and Paul, and Dicky, and Louis and Felix† as well – it's all gradually getting back to normal, the past is returning to me.

Ineke is constantly at her father's throat these days – Aunt and I hate all that quarrelling. Ineke is so unhappy, acts as if nobody loves her. But that is not true. Her parents love her, I love her very much too – and many others, if only she knew how to show her positive side, the way I know her. She thinks people don't like her – and I wish I could convince her otherwise. She finds life so difficult. It is difficult sometimes for me too, but she makes it more so for herself. The apple trees are flowering, everything is in bloom! Life is returning, everything is coming back! Hope. It's just like summer. I'm going to stop and change my

---

* Dicky Polak and his brother Rob were schoolfriends from The Hague. Marcel Adler was an acquaintance who had escaped together with Paul and had returned in the Dutch Irene Brigade.

† Louis was a classmate from the Jewish Lyceum; Felix was the husband of a cousin. He had enlisted in the Irene Brigade after escaping from prison in Spain.

clothes. Ineke has come to sit next to me and suddenly – pouf! – my inspiration is gone.

Some of the returnees, like my cousin Felix, tried to take me under their wing. But I had to show them I didn't need a guardian or adviser – I seemed to have more than enough of those.

26 April 1945

It's hard to find your way in life. You hear from all sorts of people, with all sorts of opinions, broadcasting their views. Which opinion, which viewpoint is the right one? Everyone thinks his is the right one. People try to impose their opinions and beliefs on you. If you have a father and a mother, you can ask them for advice, and listen to their ideals. Of course your own parents can try to pressure you with their opinions as well, but in my case, I would have been headed in the same direction anyway. Sometimes I'd like to be an ostrich – hide my head somewhere so that I can't see the unpleasantness of life and the ugliness of human nature – but there's no point. You have to look at the world with open eyes, and see both its good and its bad sides.

There are so many broken people in this world, so much has been smashed to pieces in this war. What I just wrote about Father and Mother, it makes one realize how lonely people are. Eventually everyone is alone and has to make his or her own way through life. Father and Mother and Jules now belong to the lovely memories of my youth. That's all over. A new world lies ahead. I'll just have to make of it what I can. To begin a new life – with Guus. I want to go and study abroad – America – and then, when I know how to do something, I'll be able to help rebuild the society of Holland.

The North was finally liberated on 5 May 1945, and the country was reunited. We celebrated wildly for the second time, but my joy was tinged with fear, apprehension – and loneliness.

4 May
Holland is free!!!!!!
5 May
It's wonderful, I have no time to write, so much has happened . . . Now Miep is free, and Nina, Uncle and Aunt and the Verhulsts, and lots of other friends. Strange, at first you go crazy with joy, with the feeling that 'home' is finally free. But then when you think about it a little more, what is awaiting you there? Mother, Father, Jules and Omi are gone. It will take a long time before you can go there again.

8 May
PEACE!
Germany has capitulated to the Allies and Russia too!!!!
Today is V-Day.
Holland is free and the war in Europe is over.
Last night I had promised the children in our street that I'd help them celebrate. So we collected the blackout paper from all the neighbours and made a bonfire with it. The parents all came out to watch. As night fell, we made a huge circle and started dancing around the fire. We were singing all sorts of songs, and some soldiers came and joined in the circle. We had a great time. My poor feet – and my poor throat! We were exhausted when we finally went to bed. But first we walked the children back to their homes, carrying paper lanterns and singing, 'Wake up! Wake up!'
Sunday we went to visit farmer Beuks, the one who helped Paul cross the border in 1942. We had a warm reception there. I was blown away by the beauty of the road on the way – a narrow path, with beautiful views, and lots of mud puddles, and the sun right ahead of me. I decided it was a fitting symbol for the reawakening of my

life: I have to skirt the puddles, and if I wobble on my bike and slip off the side of the trail, then I have to make an effort to get back on the track. With the sun ahead of you, the warm wonderful sun, and the fresh wind blowing right through you, and no one else in front of you, the road stretches out ahead, it's your very own road – and you don't have to follow anyone else.

Amsterdam is free, and so is The Hague. All the bells are ringing again. Peace at last, the peace that you have been longing for for so long. They've caught Seissie, Mussert* – all those bastards. Hitler dead, Goebbels dead – the list goes on.

PEACE!

But peace also brought with it news and pictures of the concentration camps. Peace brought terrifying confirmation of the rumours that nobody had believed possible.

14 May 1945
'What a wonderful thing it is, a mother . . .' Why do you only realize that when she's gone? How come you only understand what a mother is when she is no longer with you? . . .

You talk about your mother, as if she is no longer there. Is that the right thing to do? You just saw some pictures of Bergen-Belsen concentration camp and other camps. It was something you can never forget. Piles of exhausted corpses – thrown together in a heap, men and women, naked, almost skeletons, their faces carrying that martyred look, old people, young people, children and babies. Gallows. Ovens. German women, about twenty of them, who were supposed to 'guard' the camp. And a few survivors,

---

* General Seyss-Inquart was the German governor-general of the Netherlands; Mussert the leader of the Dutch Nazis.

horrible to look at, with legs that looked like they were walking on their own fingers – living corpses, or worse, is what those people looked like (those were the workers). After seeing that, then you don't have any reason to believe that Mother will come back some day, and how can you begrudge her the peace that she may have found? You just can't figure out what exactly you should hope for.

And today Mother would have been fifty-one years old.

A week later, Guus finally visited Breda on leave. At first we gaped at each other in wonder. My brother had changed from the flabby youth I had seen off at the docks in 1940 into a hardened soldier, a real man – a grinning American. We had not seen each other in five years. I was nineteen years old, a grown young woman. For both of us, it was like waking up from a hundred years' sleep. At first we were quite shy with each other. We were wary of saying too much about Mother, Omi and Jules. I showed him some of Mother and Father's last letters. I tried to paint as positive a picture as I could of the last time I saw Father. Guus did not cry, but paced around the zur Kleinsmiedes' dining-room table, punching his fist into the GI cap he held clenched in his other hand. He could only stay a few hours, but he promised he'd be back soon.

Mr Koperberg showed up unexpectedly at our house after being released from Westerbork. After Breda had been liberated and the push to the North was stalled at the big rivers, the Koperbergs had been flushed from their hiding place in the Biesbosch when the entire region was evacuated and deliberately flooded. Mr Koperberg had been caught, but his wife and daughter found shelter at the house of a doctor in Gorkum. We had just had a card from them before Mr Koperberg arrived, and his relief and joy when he heard that they were safe were enormous. Cousin Paul was able to travel to The Hague, and Nina and he lost no time announcing their engagement. Finally I had news of all my friends – the Fernandes and Verhulst families had all survived the famine in the North. They had eaten mashed tulip bulbs and sugar beets at the end, when potatoes had grown scarcer than gold. I had a letter from Adrie telling me he too was engaged to be married. I was not surprised – our relationship had been over for a year. I wrote to tell him I was very happy for him.

Even though I was counselled by the doctor to stop working at the evacuee shelter for a while because I was anaemic and exhausted, I tried to act happy and normal, because I had no right to feel bad – I had had it so easy, compared to what others had been through!

21 May 1945

What you hear about the camps in Germany and Poland is horrible! Two girls were at the van Buerens' who managed to escape with the help of a non-Jewish boy. Burn marks were branded on their arms, prison numbers. They had to burn their fellow victims alive and haul them away. What's left for those girls (twenty and twenty-one years old) now that they are back in normal life, with people who can sympathize, but can never comprehend the hell that they have lived through? They must have changed so much, those 'returnees from hell', they can't possibly feel at home in this petty, small-minded world. They don't have a home any more, everything is gone except the two of them, and inside them, too, everything must have been smashed to pieces by those brutes. What's worse? To survive that hell and have to continue living among people who cannot understand what that was like, or to die out there – to have peace at last?

Today is the second day of Whitsun. They are not allowing anyone north yet, unless you are in the military.

I am dying for a change, for the North, to work for the future. ('Well, what are you going to do?' you ask . . . and now I know – finally, the big decision: journalism!) I long so very much for Mother, for Guus, for Jules, all the familiar faces and places, and I so want to begin something new, finally. See now, Edith, how small-minded you are – those girls who returned from the camps can't possibly identify with your insignificant little problems!

In one of his last letters, Father had written: 'Don't ever let hate, in whatever form, overpower your soul, because nothing good has ever come of it. Hate is a disease that only brings out the same – but stronger – in others.' Much as I wanted to follow his advice, it was hard not to feel hatred under the circumstances.

1 July 1945

This afternoon I had an unexpected visit from Martin Meyer, Otto's brother* – he had seen my name on a list. We never met, but he recognized my name. He has been through hell. He spent the entire afternoon telling me about it – and I felt as if I no longer belonged to the civilized world, but was living in hell with him. Otto was with him for a long time, but in the end Otto, the stronger and bigger of the two brothers, succumbed to pneumonia. If you get sick there, they just let you die a slow death. Martin survived by working as little as possible – that was his salvation, because those who worked too hard, died. Hardly any food. If you fell ill, chances were you'd be sent to the gas chambers. Of the 230 people in his transport, there were about thirty survivors. He was forced to flee Auschwitz ahead of the Russians, then the Americans. Those final evacuations, wretched transports, cost the most lives. He doesn't under-

---

* The Meyer brothers were distant cousins from Groningen.

stand himself how he managed to survive. After a transport that lasted seven days, without any food, they arrived in Belsen and didn't get any food there either. After two days the British arrived and they were freed. Martin, weak as he was, had to carry cadavers, there were huge piles of corpses, it was a terrible camp. Then the British came with their food and it damaged their stomachs – terrible diarrhoea. They couldn't take all that heavy fatty food. Many people died from it. He couldn't tell me anything about Jules, but he did say that Jules will not return. To be in Birkenau when you are ill,* that means certain death. Gas or incineration. Also, all the older people who were deported before 1944 are all dead, according to him. They were all gassed. Some burned alive. There's not much hope for Mother, and we won't be seeing Uncle Julius or Aunt Henny either.

People, healthy young people, if there was no room for them, were simply burned alive.

Oh, isn't it terrible – if only we could pay back those executioners, that entire wretched nation. Murderers, worse than murderers they are.

I never realized that there could be such suffering in the world, and that anyone could live through it.

It was not long after this that I received the official notification from the Red Cross. Mother and Omi were confirmed to have been on a cattle truck bound for Sobibor extermination camp that had left Westerbork on 25 May 1943. Upon arrival at the camp three days later, every single survivor of that transport had been sent straight to the gas chambers.

As for Jules, it was confirmed that after his second escape

---

* I had just had a letter from an acquaintance, Ies Spetter, who had been with Jules in Birkenau and told me Jules had fallen ill there.

attempt from Westerbork, he had been sentenced to hard labour. He was sent to Birkenau on 9 March 1943 and died a year later in Auschwitz on 29 February 1944.*

* I later found out that the odds had been very much against them. Of 60,000 people who were sent to Auschwitz–Birkenau from Holland, 500 returned. Of the 34,000 whose destination had been Sobibor, only nineteen survived.

25

Picking up the Pieces

Now that we knew that Mother and Jules were not coming back, there was no reason for me to stay in Breda. Even Aunt Tine had to acknowledge that – regretfully.

20 June 1945
I've been in The Hague! I had a permit to travel from the 8th to the 15th of June. First over the Moerdijk, to take Oma* to Lisse. Door-to-door in a Red Cross van. It took us seven hours. Then a friend drove me to The Hague. Everyone amazed to see me. I was in our house twice, and it could be much worse. The Vriens† now have *nine* children. Without realizing it I crossed a minefield to get there. I managed to get into the fortress‡ without being stopped. Found quite a few of our things back in the house.

The visit to the house in de Mildestraat was a bittersweet experience. After dreaming of home for three years, I was torn by conflicting emotions as I let myself in through the front door. My feet rang hollow on the uncarpeted floor.

---

* Aunt Tine's mother from the town of Lisse, who had been on a visit to Breda at the time of our liberation, and had been trapped there until the rest of Holland was freed.
† Catholic neighbours two doors down from us.
‡ Our neighbourhood had been evacuated by the Germans as a designated 'fortress'.

Downstairs the furniture was all gone. All that remained was some cracked and chipped dishes, crumpled paper strewn in the corners, and the huge oak dresser in the dining room. When I was little, I used to throw the crusts of my bread behind that dresser when Mother wasn't looking.

In my parents' bedroom, the heavy wardrobe had not been taken either. They had probably not been able to manoeuvre these large pieces through the narrow doorways in order to haul them back to Germany.

All the woodwork was still intact, unlike in the houses of our evacuated neighbours, which had been stripped down to the bricks for firewood during the 'hunger' winter. Apparently the officer who moved in in 1942 and who took the furnishings with him, had stayed until the very end.

Finally I reached my room, on the top floor. I pushed open the door – and I couldn't believe my eyes! There was my bed. And my desk and chair, dresser and cupboard, all intact. The whole matching set, a girl's bedroom, lacquered a glossy salmon-pink. Even the beige-and-pink curtains at the window had not been touched. I could not understand it. Why was my furniture not taken? Wasn't it worth anything to them, then? Or did they simply forget about my room, on the third floor of the house? Then I noticed that my precious collection of glass animals was gone, as were my pictures, my books, my treasures. The shelves were bare.

I walked over to the window, and looked down into the street, where I used to play with the neighbourhood gang. The street, too, looked very different. A lot of trees had been cut down. The little front and back gardens looked wild and dangerously overgrown.

It was in the attic space adjoining my room that I found the other things the Germans did not have any use for. Flung in an untidy pile were our albums – the family photographs and the anniversary tributes, lavishly illustrated and lovingly penned. Boxes of documents and letters. My father's sketch-books, some etchings, and Father's palette, all encrusted with dried-up oils. Also half a dozen framed lithographs by the artist Käthe Kollwitz and her charcoal self-portrait inscribed to Father with the words 'To my dear friend David van Hessen'. I was surprised they had not destroyed these – perhaps the officer who lived in our house was not aware who the artist was. The Nazis had condemned Kollwitz's work as 'degenerate' some years before the war.

I walked back to my room and sat down on my bed. Everything was the same as before, yet it was so different. Why? I asked myself. Why was *my* furniture spared? Why *my* room? Why *me*?

Aunt Jetty and Uncle Lex Fernandes, whose own house had been gutted, soon moved into our house in de Mildestraat. 'Our home will always be your home,' they said. When Guus said we should deed the house over to them, it was not a hard decision. I was going to be a student, living in digs – what use was an empty house to me, with all its memories?

The autumn of 1945 found me enrolled at the University of Amsterdam. I changed my mind one last time about my future: even though I loved writing, I decided that psychology would be a better career than journalism, because I wanted to 'help others'. During the first year initiation rites, I was invited to join a female student society, DIS, which led to new and lasting friendships. I soon joined the women's varsity rowing team, which was to win the national university championships in 1947. That year I was president of the women's rowing club.

Although I sometimes found it hard to get through the day, I would not allow myself to be sad. It was a new world, and I knew what was required of me – to see the sunny side, to make the best of things; to turn over a new leaf. The following letter, written to one of my college friends, expresses my mood at that time.

The Hague, 27 December '46
Dear Maro,*

You know I am not sombre. I know I often make that impression on you, but that may be an unconscious reaction to the feeling I often have when I'm with you: that you expect it of me. Always, when I'm with young people who have not been as affected by the war, they seem to want to feel sorry for me, or at least sympathy. And that is normal, but then I feel such a hypocrite, because I am not sad any more – whatever people think.

Before he died, Father tried to prepare me gradually for what would happen. Mother was already gone and so was Jules. We two were the only ones left. He on his deathbed in Utrecht, and I in Breda. But everyone, Maro, has had their own problems. Whether you were Jewish or not, everyone had their own burden to bear. When you mourn the dead, what you are really mourning for is the survivors, and that means Guus and myself. And we are richer than some people who have not lost anybody, but who did not have such parents. And it is good that Father died. That way he was spared much suffering and pain. What happened to Mother I don't know. I cannot imagine it either. For me she will always be the sturdy, attractive, kind, vivacious woman who used to sit by my bed when I was little; who consoled me in my childish sorrows and who later was like a friend to me. When I first saw photos of the mountains of corpses in the concentration camps, I could not imagine that Mother was one of them. Perhaps that has been my good fortune. Jules was my best friend and I can't imagine

---

* Marijke (Maro) Hofland-Peters.

him either, at the end, what it was like for him. I now often feel them close by, just as always – they were always there for me.

And I feel so strong, Maro, because they wanted me to be strong. But then, every time you realize that someone is feeling sorry for you, it's like an undeserved consolation prize. Even that delicate avoidance of the words 'Father' and 'Mother' – that always bothers me. If someone asks, 'Are your parents still alive?', I'll say, 'No,' and then, suddenly, that fastidious silence, and no one knows where to look.

You know, Maro, it is not just about me. But people should not allow themselves to forget how people have been annihilated in this war. And they should not just think about the people they knew, e.g. 'those good, decent Jews' or 'those people who, though Jewish, were good respectable people nevertheless'. They should think about a portion of mankind that was annihilated by fellow human beings. And whether it was Jew or Christian or heathen, whether it's 1946 or 1843 or 200 BC; it's always the same thing, this inhumanity, this bestiality. That is what we should all remember. Even if we think, 'It is the destiny of our world,' we should fight to make it better. It's true, Maro, I agree that deep down we are good. That in all of us there simmers something that we had when we came into this world: something good, something warm, something to do with love.

Before the war, when the canals froze over and you saw all the people carrying their skates, with red cheeks and all invigorated by the cold, and I walked around in my baggy trousers with a comfy old windcheater on, I could have danced right there in the street – I felt at one with all the people. I used to walk around and wish I could be a child for ever, to start conversations with anyone and everyone, to ride a bike like a boy. And when you're in town and every passer-by is cheerful or someone says something funny, then you come home with that warm feeling: how wonderful life is. Does that happen to you sometimes, that you are so full of love that you don't know what to do with it all?

I'm babbling on, excuse me. But this afternoon, on my bike, the sun was so warm and the trees looked so beautiful against the blue sky and the people were walking so cheerfully in the street and the sun kept shining and you had told me in your letter that you were happy and your life was good . . . and then I knew: it is true, not everyone is bitter. Not everything has been destroyed in the war. There are still plenty of people with ideals, people who know how to be happy.

You asked me about Christmas. Well, no . . . for us it was Chanuleah. Our feast of light at home, on Friday nights, we used to have two candelabra on the table, and Mother would light the candles when it got dark and then she'd wave her hands over the candles and say the blessing: 'Blessed is the eternal holy God who has made the light.' Then Father would break the bread (a challah bread), bless it and give us each a piece of it, sprinkled with salt. After the meal it was always 'our' Friday evening, when we were together as a family. We would make music or sing, or Father would read to us from Shakespeare, Goethe, Heine, Edgar Allan Poe, etc. Sometimes we'd dance, and it was always wonderful. We were liberal Jews and followed our religion in our own way. Now do you understand, Maro, why Christmas means nothing to me? I mean, it does have some meaning for me, but not the way it has for you, with the baby Jesus and the crib. There is a lot in the Jewish religion that's beautiful. I never knew much about it but I hope to learn more. And I swear that what happened during the inauguration will never happen again: I mean when we all asked each other about our religious beliefs, and when you asked me what I believed in, I said, 'Nothing'. Because at that moment I had no beliefs. But now I believe in goodness, above all. And the beauty of life, and the beauty in people. And after that, I feel that I am Jewish. That I will always keep that religion and that we who are believers, whatever our religion may be, are obliged to continue it.

I volunteered at a Jewish children's home and took over as interim director for a while when the director set off with a group of orphans on a clandestine trip to the Middle East. (Smuggling Jewish children into Palestine was illegal under British rule.) It was at this time that I first met Loet Velmans again, who had been a classmate of Jules before the war. He had just returned from a Japanese prisoner-of-war camp, and was reed-thin; his skin still had the yellow cast of malaria. He too was a survivor, although his experience had been very different from mine. Like me, he was a student at Amsterdam University.

Our friendship developed slowly but surely. Loet, being a decisive person, was soon convinced that I was the girl for him, but it wasn't until I had fulfilled another promise to myself (to go to America to study; I completed a year's post-graduate work at Columbia University in 1948–9) that I made up my mind to marry him. With Loet I created a new family, to replace the one I had lost. Our marriage has been a happy one and has lasted close to fifty years.

Ineke was enrolled in the University of Leiden. I introduced her to one of my first cousins, Dolf van Hessen, who had just qualified as an architectural engineer in Delft. Dolf had made it through the war by being hidden on a farm. Ineke felt she already knew Dolf, from the stories I had told her about all my cousins while we were standing at the kitchen sink doing the dishes. I was happy to see that the two of them hit it off right away.

When Nina Fernandes married my cousin Paul and became Nina van Hessen, and when Ineke zur Kleinsmiede married Dolf and became Ineke van Hessen, I understood that we had all come full circle. The two families who had helped me survive, who had been my parents' lifeline in their darkest hour, were now my family, related to me by marriage. My name – just one of the millions of names silenced, forged, hidden or wiped out in the war – was to be their children's and grandchildren's name. It seemed a fitting end to our story.

Afterword

Tine zur Kleinsmiede was widowed in 1946, when her husband Egbert died from complications following a hernia operation. A few years later, Job zur Kleinsmiede (Egbert's brother, also widowed) became her second husband. Gradually, over the years, Aunt Tine and I grew even closer, although she assured me always that she never wanted to take the place of my mother.

In 1983, to celebrate her ninetieth birthday, I took her to Israel, where she was honoured as a 'Righteous Gentile' at the Holocaust Memorial 'Yad Vashem'. We had kept the ceremony a complete surprise from her until the last minute. After planting a tree in the 'Forest of the Righteous' overlooking the hills of Judea, she said she was happy to have gained a daughter and had only one regret: that she and her husband had not been able to save the Gokkes family.

She told the assembled officials that what she had done was nothing special: 'Anyone would have done the same thing, in my place. Any *decent* person, that is.'

Tine died in 1994. She was one hundred years old.